RIPPLE MAKER

TEACHING EFFECTIVELY AND LOVING IT!

Davis Laughlin

Published by Davis Laughlin, Ltd.

Editing assistance provided by Renata Herrmann, Amber Fetters, Tara Laughlin and Tracy Wilson.

Special thanks to my wife, Donna Laughlin, and my two grown children, Amber Fetters and Tara Laughlin. Amber is a middle school teacher and Tara is a CPA. I am blessed.

Very special thanks to my grandchildren, Averie, Meredith and Caleb, who have given me a new set of educational eyes.

Table of Contents

Introduction

"The best teachers become the best teachers by being their own best students."
Laurie Gray

Splat! The gooey spitball hit my crotch and fell to the tile floor in my middle school science classroom. It was the very first class period of a brand new school year. I had never met the twenty-five seventh grade students who were now staring my way with wide eyes.

Although none were saying a word, they were all wondering something like, "What is this teacher (who I do not know yet) going to do about that spitball?" Trevor, the offender, looked proud of his aim for a split second before his face lost all of its color and took on the ashen appearance of a convicted criminal awaiting sentencing.

I taught for 27 years before the spitball incident and certainly was not expecting to learn anything new that day. However, in an amazing way, that moment and the moments immediately thereafter, helped me see how far I had come as an educator and lit a fire inside me that changed the course of my career.

What was the reason for this epiphany? How could a disrespectful, disobedient student in the first minutes of a new school year ignite such a spark with a well-aimed spitball to the crotch?

Most instructive to me were the things I <u>DID NOT</u> do in the seconds immediately after the spitball fell to the floor.

- Act shocked or flustered

- Show panic

- Become angry

- Try to prove my authority

- Get even with the disrespectful, young cuss

- Belittle the offender

- Make an example out of Trevor

- Holler

- Glare

- Send the young man to the office

- Ask angrily, "Who shot this?"

- Say, "No one leaves this room until I find out who did this!"

- Assign a detention

- Go off on a 20-minute rant about behavior

What I <u>DID</u> at that moment was equally telling:

- I looked down at the spitball on the floor at my feet.

- I paused for a few seconds to think.

- I looked up at the class, and then at Trevor, and smiled. It
was a genuine smile, not a sarcastic, evil grin.

- I simply said that we would be talking about appropriate

behavior in this classroom later and this spitball was an example of something that was not appropriate.

- Then calmly and still with a smile, I asked Trevor if he could please come and throw the spitball in the trash, which he was more than eager to do by this time.
- I thanked Trevor for helping me get the year started with such an interesting activity.

I did not crush Trevor with my teacher power, which was surely a reasonable option. I did not ignore the situation either. I had that class, and Trevor, in the palm of my hand for the rest of the year. It was amazing.

Had this incident happened in my fifth year of teaching I am certain I would not have handled it like I did in my twenty-seventh. I would have most certainly chosen a different path of action. In fact, had this happened in even my fifteenth year I am sure I would have reacted in a way that would have involved punishment for or revenge on Trevor.

I would have made sure every student knew that this was my classroom, that I was the king and in that capacity was also the dispenser of all wisdom, truth and discipline. I would have made sure those students saw that I had more power than they did and that I was not afraid to use it.

I saw Trevor in the high school parking lot last week, six years had elapsed since the historical spitball. He and his classmates were pulling off their version of the annual senior prank by turning part of the high school parking lot into a beach scene. It was a cool idea, in my opinion. After all, we live in Kansas.

I was at the high school that day, waiting for our busses of eighth graders to load back up following an end-of-the-year promotion practice. Trevor walked over with the biggest smile on his now-whiskered face. He shook my hand and grinned. I returned both.

Trevor proceeded to tell me that one of his final assignments as a high school senior was to write a paper about his most memorable moment in school over the years. You know where this is going. We were both grinning from ear to ear as he recounted writing the paper and describing the spitball scene from his perspective. I did the same from mine. Then he said, "Mr. Laughlin, I will never forget that moment." There was a long pause, then a quiet, "Or you. Thanks for everything." I was glad I was wearing sunglasses.

Tears filled my eyes as I gave Trevor a hug and wished him the best in the days ahead. I hoped I would see Trevor again someday, remembering the hundreds of students I have not seen since their own high school graduations.

Trevor was a rowdy student, one of those young boys who seemed to enjoy watching a teacher lose his or her cool. He also enjoyed playing the part of the class clown. He was good at it. There were probably ten or more reasons Trevor thought it would be a good idea to shoot me in the crotch with a spitball that day.

The longer I teach, the more I see that a large majority of poor behavior is a disguise for what is often a difficult learning problem, family situation, personal struggle, stress or just a bad day. I am sure none of Trevor's purposes that day were to guarantee I would make a real connection with him throughout his middle school years and now onward into his life, but that is exactly what happened.

As that spitball fell to my feet a few years ago, I realized several things about myself as a teacher. From a student's perspective, those insights would have been in question form.

- Is Mr. Laughlin able to manage or control this classroom?

- What is Mr. Laughlin like as a person? Is he going to explode? Is he going to ignore the spitball? (Neither of those choices would have worked well for any of us.)

- Will I matter in this classroom as a person? Will I be just another student in just another class?

- Am I going to like this class? Will the classroom atmosphere help me want to learn?

- Is Mr. Laughlin comfortable around us? Can he be himself or does he put on a teacher mask like most other teachers?

- Does Mr. Laughlin force obedience and respect? Does he seem to like his students?

At that moment in that first class of the year, when things could not have been much worse for a teacher, a spitball defined my career. That moment made a difference in Trevor's life and in mine.

I often wonder if Trevor would have finished high school had I ripped into him that morning. That spitball did not just help me see teaching in a clearer way, it did not just affect Trevor and his classmates forever, it also cast a ripple that is affecting you as you read this book. Trevor left his handprint on my heart. I hope I left something of myself with him.

Each day in classrooms everywhere, teachers create ripples in the lives of their students, like rocks dropped into a pond. Some ripples are positive and some are negative. Teachers cannot have a neutral effect on their students. The ripples spread and never really disappear. Our rock makes a splash and falls to the bottom of the pond every day. Each new day our rocks are lifted back up and are dropped again. Lives are affected for good, for bad and forever.

Over the course of my final years in the classroom, I began to develop a passion for educators. Do not get me wrong; I still love young people and enjoy developing young minds. But for reasons I do not totally understand, I now have a dream of spending the rest of my life encouraging, challenging and transforming educators everywhere. My dream is that more teachers will become positive and influential 'ripple makers' through my presentations and this book.

I do not want teachers to continue struggling along, frustrated and discouraged, dreading each new day. Being a teacher should mean so much more than it often does. Before we begin, let me throw out a few things to remember:

1 – No educational book, whether theoretical or practical in nature, will solve all your problems or make you the perfect teacher. The teaching/learning process is so complicated and involves so many variables that no single expert's strategies or research-based data could ever work for all teachers, students or schools every day or even any day. No matter what we do and how we do it, there are times we fail. Teaching is hard. This book will not be the solution to your every teaching need; although I sure hope it will address many of them.

2 – I have written this book to be used as a workbook. Write in it. There are pages for notes at the end. Cross out the parts you do not like. Highlight the ones you would like to try. My hope is that

school staffs will also use it as a practical book study.

3 – Of course, no one can teach nearly 40 years without being influenced by a great number of people. So, in a sense, this book is not just dedicated to all the current and future teachers in our classrooms today, but to those who have gone before me or have worked alongside me. There are simply too many people to list here, but you all know who you are. Thanks so much.

Chapter One: Setting the Stage

"It is the supreme art of the teacher to awaken joy in creative expression and knowledge."
Albert Einstein

I know about you. You are an educator. You work hard and make a difference in the lives of students, but you also get tired and frustrated. The pressures and requirements of your job are wearing on you. The joy you once had is fading. You might be sensing yourself becoming disillusioned and cynical. Managing your classroom is getting harder. You might be feeling like you just are not reaching some of your students.

You are tired of all the meetings, lesson plans and high stakes testing. I know about you. I was you. Actually, I still am you.

I spent 33 years as a classroom teacher and although the large majority of that time was in my middle school science classroom, I either taught or coached at every grade level from kindergarten to graduate classes at the university level, where I am currently teaching. I know tired. I understand frustration.

I felt the pressure of high stakes testing. I had lessons that failed. I taught with negative colleagues and had moments of negativity myself. If there is anyone who could actually ever help you rediscover the passion you once had for teaching and give you a few practical tips that will transform your teaching, it would probably be me.

This book is an attempt to encourage and support the dedicated and sometimes desperate educators who have the huge responsibility of molding young lives. In the hands of a committed educator, this book could very well change the direction and effectiveness of an entire teaching career. I hope it does just that for you. The last thing we need is for educators like you to leave the profession.

Currently, nearly 50% of new teachers leave the classroom by their fifth year. When asked why they left, these frustrated teachers cited a lack of administrative support, difficulties with student discipline, and low salary levels as major reasons for their exodus.[i]

The demands keep increasing and too often the support is lacking. Instead of being encouraged, teachers are becoming discouraged. More than anything else I hope this book brings a huge dose of encouragement to educators everywhere.

In the next few decades, humanity will face some of the greatest challenges we have ever faced. If we are not able to deal with these challenges effectively, we are all in trouble. Who will be responsible for making the majority of the future's worldly decisions? Yes, you are correct; today's youth will be tomorrow's leaders. These young people MUST learn and learn well.

They must learn how to think, not just what to think. They

must develop a diverse set of skills with enough flexibility to adjust in our rapidly changing world. How are these youngsters going to reach the levels of competence on which the future of humanity depends?

The all-important answer is great teaching: influential teaching, powerful teaching, effective teaching. There has never been a time in history when the importance of teaching is as critical as it is at this moment.

The odds are good that you are one of the critical mass. It is not enough to be a dedicated teacher anymore. You must be effective – highly effective. You must be constantly striving to improve your craft.

But to become truly effective as an educator, it is imperative that you also fall in love with the challenge and that you rediscover the joy and passion you once had for this vital career.

Dr. Todd Whitaker, a Professor of Educational Leadership at Indiana State University, author and well-known motivational speaker, hits the nail on the head when he says, "The best thing about being a teacher is that it matters. The hardest thing about being a teacher is that it matters every day."[iii] Whitaker often shares that people are the key component in schools, not programs. Great schools are made up of great teachers.

One of the problems with education today is the constant addition of new programs, standards, curricula, tools, strategies and reforms. For some reason, many administrators and legislators think outdated curricula, misguided programs and a lack of technological tools are the problem.

So it is no surprise that these same educational leaders also think new programs, standards, curricula, and technology are the solution. When will educators realize those things are never the answer? People are the problem and have always been so. People are also the solution.

Think of the last program your school implemented. Was that program the answer to your school's challenges? Again, Whitaker says it best, "The reason programs don't work is because whatever the new program is, the ineffective people can't do that one either." What program can fix ineffective teachers?

What usually happens with a new program anyway? The best teachers embrace it, value it and put it into practice, but the poor teachers either can't or won't, so the program is eventually cut and a new one is added."[iii]

There are some experts who claim that effective teachers are born, not made - that those teachers have some special genetic trait. There are others with the opposite view that effective teachers are made, not born, through years of experience and training. I am sure the truth lies somewhere in the middle in some shade of gray.

This book is written in gray shades. It will have thoughts and strategies that fit your natural gifts and skills, and it will have thoughts and strategies you can learn to use. This book will make a positive difference in the effectiveness of the educators who read it. It can and will improve your teaching.

Over the past few years, I have been honored with several teaching awards. My live appearance on the *Live with Regis and Kelly* TV show as one of the top five teachers in the United States was certainly exciting.[iv] People tell me it is obvious I was born to be a teacher. I am grateful for the natural personality quirks and gifts that are helpful to me as an educator; however, I was just a mediocre teacher for too many years.

My classroom management skills were weak, my ability to reach all my students was poor, and I had little understanding of various instructional strategies, brain research or a variety of assessment tools. I nearly quit teaching after my first year because I just did not feel cut out to be a teacher. I was ineffective and I knew it.

My first principal, Mr. Seaton, was gracious enough to give me another chance and I owe a lot to him for that. For some reason, I stuck it out. Gradually, I started to learn how to be an effective teacher and the more effective I became, the more I enjoyed teaching.

I read books, I went to conferences, I stayed awake during some in-service presentations and, most importantly, I watched the great teachers at my school. I had several dedicated administrators who all helped challenge and shape me as an educator.

I did not like some of their suggestions at the time, but I tried most of them and some of them actually worked. I started adding tools and trying new strategies, and after a few years, my effectiveness started growing.

Over the course of the last ten years of my career, our district built a new middle school and I moved into that building with some of the best educators I have ever seen. I must admit that if there is any excellence to my teaching, it happened as a result of my colleagues' greatness over the years.

Thanks especially to Shawnda, who opened my eyes to creative ways to teach and assess learning. Marty, a long-time friend and colleague, has challenged and sharpened my thinking about education more than anyone. Paula and I taught so long together we became like family. I could name so many others who have cast personal and professional ripples into my life and career. I am forever grateful.

When a teacher works with other effective educators in an atmosphere of mutual respect and humility, the best is brought out of all involved.

I share these thoughts in this opening chapter to encourage you. You can become a truly effective teacher even if you are not one now. I know that from personal experience. If you are already a great teacher, you can still find ways to improve your craft and you should.

In his book, *Talent is Overrated*, Geoff Colvin tells the story of the Beatles.ᵛ Although it is obvious those lads were born with some musical ability, it was their hard work and persevering attitudes that developed their musical genius.

The Beatles played every night of the week in Hamburg, usually for five or more hours at a stretch for two straight years. If you listen to any of the Beatles' music from that period, you understand why so many record studios turned them down. But they kept at it. They worked hard, improved and a few years down the road became one of the history's greatest bands.

Effective teachers take full responsibility for the learning that occurs in their classrooms. They don't blame last year's teacher. They don't blame the student's parents. They do not blame the divorce rate or the economy. These teachers blame themselves if students fail.

Students will fail from time to time, but a great teacher focuses on his or her response to student failure, not just on the failure itself.

Great teachers care. They truly understand their students. These influential teachers have a confidence to be themselves around their students. Young people are not clueless. Students sense any little fake or insecure vibe teachers give.

Effective, influential teachers do not just show a passion for their subject matter, they show a passion for young people and have an empathy that allows them to value the backgrounds of every student.

I am getting ahead of myself here. Please join me as I show you some of the secrets I have found in my 34 years as a teacher. I tried very hard to make this book readable, practical and encouraging - and short.

You could be grading papers, working on lesson plans or taking a nap, but you have decided to spend your valuable time with me. Thanks. You will not regret it. Your teaching may never be the same.

Other References: Chapter One

Colvin, Geoff. *Talent Is Overrated.* Portfolio Trade, 2010. Print.

Darling-Hammond, L. "Teachers and teaching: Testing policy hypotheses from national commission report." *Educational Researcher, (1998):* 5-15.

Gonzalez, Liza, Michelle Brown, and John Slate. *Teachers Who Left the Teaching Profession: A Qualitative Understanding.* www.nova.edu. The Qualitative Report, March 2008. Web. July 2011.

Whitaker, Todd. *What Great Teachers Do Differently.* Eye on Education, 2003. Print.

Chapter Two: Feeling the Pressure

"There's a terrible price to pay for stress in your life - it really takes a hit on your heart."
Leeza Gibbons

Teachers feel the strain. More responsibility is being heaped onto teachers' shoulders and little, if any, is ever removed. Test scores, governmental pressure, accountability issues, international comparisons, and societal burdens are in headlines every day.

The Sandy Hook Elementary School shootings and the Moore, Oklahoma tornado disaster occurred during the editing phase of this book. Those tragedies, like others before it, demonstrate the compassion most teachers have and the countless responsibilities they face each day.

The majority of teachers I know are hard-working, dedicated professionals in spite of their current stress levels. The pressure educators feel today is greater than at any other time in American education. I hope this book encourages teachers and provides them with strategies and practices that will alleviate some of that stress and return more smiles to more faces.

High stakes pressure on schools is nothing new. Schools and teachers have been under scrutiny for as long as education has been compulsory, which in some New England colonies began in the 17th century.[vi] My own lifetime is full of interesting educational reform. One particularly historical event stands out as a great example.

I was born on September 4, 1957. Sputnik was in orbit exactly a month later. The launch of Sputnik embarrassed America and triggered several fearful reactions. America's reaction was swift and purposeful. The race to space became a priority in an attempt to keep pace with, and eventually surpass, the scientific advancements of the Soviets. Our freedom was at risk. If the Soviet Union could launch satellites, it could launch ballistic missiles that could carry nuclear weapons.

The launching of Sputnik shook the security of Americans and prompted fear that America's educational system had failed. American opinion attributed Sputnik's success to the Soviet educational system and placed the blame for America's alarming second-place position in the arms and space races on its failing schools and universities.

Critics of America's school systems popped up everywhere. Something had to be done. For the first time, the federal government fastened its grip on America's schools and expanded its influence on educational policies that were traditionally determined by the states.

Thomas N. Bonner, in a 1957 issue of *The Journal of Higher Education* stated, "It is upon education that the fate of our way of life depends."[vii] Bonner was not alone in his beliefs. People concluded that

American's system of education was disorganized and undemanding. America had fallen behind the dreaded Soviets and education was to blame.

As a result, the federal government seized control of all levels of American education for the first time and poured millions of dollars into science education, engineering and mathematics. In 1958, President Dwight D. Eisenhower signed the *National Aeronautics and Space Act*, establishing NASA.

The National Science Foundation's funding was tripled and more young Americans were encouraged to go into fields of science and engineering.[viii] The pressure was on teachers and schools. It was not the first time education was the target of societal pressure and it clearly was not the last.

Since Sputnik, there have been numerous school reforms; Nation at Risk, Goals 2000, No Child Left Behind and Race to the Top are among the most recognizable. There have been others, many others, and each new one that appears on the horizon is hailed by zealous, but misinformed governmental officials and educators as the magic bullet.

New curricular movements sprang up along the way as well. The latest, Common Core Standards, could cost my home state of Kansas over 60 million dollars to incorporate over the next five years.[ix] California's Common Core Standards implementation could exceed 1.5 billion dollars.

Have all these reforms and curricula fixed our educational issues? The question must be asked by everyone who has a stake in education today: parents, teachers, students, taxpayers and legislators.

In 2012 alone, the U.S. federal government spent over 100 billion dollars on education; however, the majority of education money comes from state and local governments. America spends over $7,000 per student each year for education, and that number will continue to rise.[x]

School reforms and updated curricula have undoubtedly improved various aspects of the teaching/learning process, but programs, money, technology and curriculum changes are never the real difference makers. As I mentioned earlier, it is teachers who are the critical variable in classrooms and schools.

The magic of teaching is produced using a recipe of insight, communication, and personal connections, baked in an oven of experience.

Yet instead of developing teachers' intra-personal and inter-personal skills and encouraging honest teacher reflection, school districts continue to spend huge chunks of money on programs, textbooks, technology and other secondary pieces to the education puzzle.

Throwing billions of dollars at schools will not automatically produce effective, influential teachers and most certainly will not guarantee better learning.

We can do much better. We must.

Other References: Chapter Two

Bonner, Thomas. *The Journal of Higher Education, (1957). Print.* September 2011.

Delisle, Jason. "Putting a number of federal education spending," (2013). http://economix.blogs.nytimes.com. Web. March 2013.

Millburn, John. "Kansas audit pegs cost of new ed standards," (2012). www.hutchnews.com. Web. January 2013.

Powell, Alvin. "How Sputnik changed U.S. education," (2007). www.news.harvard.edu. Web. September 2011.

USC Rossier Online Staff. "U.S. spending and performance versus the world," (2011). www.rossieronline.usc.edu. Web. September 2011.

Chapter Three: Making a Difference

"It's easy to make a buck. It's a lot tougher to make a difference."
Tom Brokaw

For those of you who have children in school, it is your perception of their teachers that shapes your opinions of that school. Students who think their teachers are quality educators also tend to think highly of their schools. If a school has a large percentage of effective teachers, it is usually considered to be a quality school. Throughout your own education, you had effective teachers and you had ineffective ones. When you had a great teacher, the entire learning process was more enjoyable and more impactful.

After parents, teachers are the most important variable in education. Sadly, for many of your students, there is little or no parental involvement in their learning, so you often become the most important piece of the puzzle. Schools cannot be effective if its teachers are not.

With that in mind, there are a couple simple ways to improve a school - hire more effective teachers and/or improve the effectiveness of the current teachers. Truly effective teachers are easy to spot. Let me share a story about a couple friends of mine who also happen to be teachers from my own district.

Our school district is a suburban district, just outside of Wichita, Kansas, and serves one of the most economically diverse student populations in the state. As this part of the state develops and grows, so does the student population in our district. The increase in student population outpaces the capacity of school buildings in a couple of sites.

One school currently uses an old, double-wide mobile home to house some students. I was substitute teaching in that school earlier this year and decided to walk out to the 'camper,' as it is affectionately called by the two classes of fourth graders and their teachers, Mrs. Luszczak and Mrs. Duncan.

I opened the door and saw an absolutely amazing learning environment in session. Some students were working in groups; a couple were working with partners, a handful with the teacher, and others independently. Everyone was excited and highly engaged. Mrs. Luszczak gave me a quick tour of the 'camper.' It is an old, drafty structure and the floor bounces when you walk, but the learning going on there was second to none.

I discovered that these two teachers volunteered to move out into the camper. This pair of dynamic educators turned this rickety, old mobile home into a magical kingdom of adventure and joy. Their students feel privileged to leave the school building, walk outside through the weather and enter the 'camper' several times a day.

Would Mrs. Luszczak or Mrs. Duncan love to have a permanent, comfortable classroom with new amenities? Sure! They would create a magical kingdom of adventure and learning there, too, no doubt. With a proper classroom, they will be even more effective and engaging.

Modern facilities do matter, no one can argue that, but not near as much as an effective teacher does. Excellent teachers are effective all the time, in any circumstance and in any environment. In any setting, great teachers inspire incredible learning and unlimited thinking.

If educational experts stopped into Mrs. Luszczak's and Mrs. Duncan's 'camper' and saw their interaction with students, they would probably require all schools to add double-wide mobile homes as classrooms. That is how many educational experts think.

These experts often conclude that it is programs, money, buildings, and curricula that produce learning. Ugh. Effective teachers can teach without textbooks, and they can teach without computers. They can teach poor students as well as those who are wealthy. Effective teachers teach well in September, and just as well in May. No assessment can ever measure an amazing teacher's impact.

I have read countless books on teaching, taken numerous workshops and classes and sat through hundreds of professional development training sessions, all which encouraged the use of new strategies, programs or curricula. Some of these were so helpful that I included them in this book. Still, no strategy, program or curriculum is the key to the magical kingdom of teaching.

Great teachers can find a way to use just about any idea or strategy and improve the learning in their classrooms. Ineffective teachers look for excuses and reasons not to try things; or even worse, have such a negative, critical attitude that improvement is the furthest goal in their minds.

Some influential teachers are strict and some are not. Many inspiring teachers give out candy while others do not. Some engaging teachers follow a textbook religiously and some never use one. A countless number of effective teachers use seating charts while some never do. Some great teachers lecture daily and some avoid lecturing at all costs. Do you see a pattern here?

The effectiveness and influence of a teacher is determined by HOW she uses a strategy or program instead of by WHAT strategy or program she uses. An effective teacher gets amazing results because of HOW he uses materials instead of WHAT materials he uses.

A great teacher just gets it. She builds lasting connections. She wants to improve. So, how do we start having more fun and being more effective at the same time? You do not have to look too far to find the starting line.

Chapter Four – Looking Inward

"An unexamined life is not worth living."
Socrates

Imagine getting ready for school without a single mirror in your house or apartment. Without mirrors, it is difficult to evaluate yourself. You cannot see if your hair looks good or not. You cannot recognize the spot you missed while shaving.

Granted, you could get a view of your clothes from your head's perspective by looking down, but that only gives you so much information. If you want to make sure you look good from head to toe, you would probably step in front of a full-length mirror. Mirrors give us a true reflection of what and who we are. They let us see all parts of ourselves accurately and without distortion.

This book is a teacher mirror. My hope for you is that while you read it, you will be challenged to see your teaching clearly and honestly. It takes some guts to look into a mirror some days. After an extended illness or a long night's sleep, your hair, face and eyes seldom look good.

I once addressed an important audience with my zipper down. A kind man finally waved at me, pointing to my pants. I laughed, zipped things up and finished my speech with a minimum of embarrassment. I have worn shirts inside out, buttoned shirts incorrectly and missed belt loops. In fact, my wife still gives me a good 'lookover' before I leave for work each day.

With the mirror as a guide, most of us brush this, wash that, shave this, apply makeup and fix our clothes. Then, we take a final look into the mirror, congratulate ourselves on how good we look and run right along into the day ahead.

Throughout this book, you will find some strategies you can use to improve your teaching, and some strategies you are already using well. Most of you will read many more of the latter.

You may have previously seen the following quote, "The unexamined life is not worth living." Socrates is one of several people throughout the ages who are credited with saying that or something similar. Supposedly, Socrates used these words at his trial for heresy. He was on trial for encouraging his students to think for themselves and to challenge the established beliefs of the time.

Socrates paid a huge price for his dedication to the importance of 'knowing thyself.' He was sentenced to death.

If we examine our teaching, we are not going to be sentenced to death, although there are days when some classes and students might make you feel like you have been. Sadly, there are many teachers who have been in the classroom for twenty or more years without ever examining their own teaching.

Most of those teachers are dedicated to their profession and have file cabinets full of worksheets, notes, computer files and lesson plans they proudly use year after year. They are doing an adequate job for most students.

Most are probably well-respected in their schools and might have even been recognized with Teacher of the Year awards. But they have never held a mirror up in front of their teaching and studied it carefully and honestly. They could be so much more effective, reach so many more students and have more fun each day.

Instead, they keep on doing what they have always done, getting the same adequate results they always get. These teachers have little or no idea how ineffective they are with many of their students. If they DID know they were ineffective, many would not care.

A number of these teachers have lost their love of teaching but are determined to survive until retirement. Their joy is gone and their students know it.

Teachers are not the only people who avoid evaluating themselves. The sad reality is that most people avoid leading an examined life. It is not that we do not have time or make time. We are just afraid of what we might see. We avoid evaluations at all costs. This happens in all aspects of life.

A person (or couple) who is in the midst of financial trouble often refuses to take a long, hard look at his or her spending. There are men and women who know they have some sort of a health issue but refuse to visit the doctor out of fear of the unknown. We tend to think that our problems will improve by themselves, and as long as we keep them hidden away, everything will work out somehow.

'Out of sight, out of mind,' is becoming the way of the world. People know they need to change, but their pride, stubbornness, laziness or apathy keep them away from the mirror. People will do anything, no matter how strange, to avoid looking deeply inside themselves.

I am not suggesting any of you need to change a thing about your teaching. Each of you could show me a few effective teaching strategies. What I am suggesting is that you turn on a bright light and stand in front of a full-length teacher mirror.

I spent a lot of time in front of that mirror during the last twenty-five years of my career. The first time I really looked at my teaching I did not like what I saw. In my new venture as university instructor, author, and professional development provider, I am facing many of those first-time errors again. The observing, analysing, evaluating and correcting never end, nor should they, in any area of life.

I encourage you to begin to know yourself on a deeper level and use that knowledge to take control of your teaching. The clearer your purposes as a teacher become, the more quickly you will recover the passion you once had and enjoy a fulfillment you may be lacking.

There is a freedom in being able to look inside yourself with a sense of honesty and humility. There is an excitement in stepping outside of the stress of your hectic classroom and considering the big picture reasons behind why you teach.   There is hope in these thoughts. It is a lot of fun, too.

Usually, the most difficult part of any journey is the first step and as you would think, the most difficult part of a self-evaluation is the start. You have to be honest; you have to be open and you have to think deeply. I think you are ready for that.

Chapter Five - Pinpointing Your Purpose

"Definiteness of purpose is the starting point of all achievement."

W. Clement Stone

About twenty years ago, most schools across the country developed mission statements. Committees formed, discussions took place and signs appeared in classrooms and office windows. Some of you participated in that process. Most of your mission statements are probably very similar to that of my own district:

> *"The Vision and Purpose of Circle USD 375, in partnership with our communities, is to educate each student to be an engaged, knowledgeable citizen and responsible, productive worker in the 21st Century."*

Mission statements should give direction and purpose for schools and districts, but let's be honest: few educators use their district or school mission statement to guide their planning and instruction. Few administrators and school board members consider mission statements when planning or guiding the educational process even though they should.

The next new educational fad pushed mission statements into the background. Educators forgot they had a mission. That is too bad. A mission statement is a very useful tool for a district, school and its teachers. But let me ask you, do you have a *personal* mission statement?

Dr. Stephen Covey, in his best-selling book, *Seven Habits of Highly Effective People,* titles his second habit, *Begin with the End in Mind.*[xi] Covey goes on to encourage readers to "self-discover and clarify your deeply important character values and life goals. Envision the ideal characteristics for each of your various roles and relationships in life."

Have you ever written down what is important to you in your teaching career? Have you defined your own unique purpose(s) as an educator and felt the incredible satisfaction that comes from fulfilling that purpose(s)? Most teachers do not have a mission statement. They do not have a specific reason for teaching.

Most of us just get up early each day, go to our classrooms, teach all day, go home and repeat. This continues year after year, decade after decade. Then one day we stop and realize we spent 30 years on a teacher treadmill and are not sure why.

I spent many years on that treadmill before I stepped off and evaluated what I was doing and why I was doing it. Many teachers are thrown off this treadmill each year and never recover.

When I took the time to think deeply about my teaching I began to see the 'big picture reasons' for my work with young people. I became less frustrated with the smaller details and hassles of my job and started enjoying planning lessons and interacting with students and colleagues much more.

Copy machine malfunctions, staff meetings, late papers, and fire drills no longer drained my battery. The more clearly I defined my purposes as a teacher, the more effective educator I became.

In my involvement in my community and church, several families have asked me to speak at funeral services. I have spent many hours with these families in their times of grief in an attempt to get enough memories to honor the life of the deceased family member through a quality eulogy or message.

Preparing for a funeral service is not fun or easy. However, if I can get a real sense of the deceased man or woman's interests, dreams, struggles and joys, capturing and celebrating a well-lived life falls into place. If I knew the person well, it is an even greater advantage.

If I was speaking at your funeral, what would you want me to say about you as a teacher? What mattered most to you during your career? What was important to you? Where did you put your energy and passion? What gave you satisfaction and fulfillment? What was the main reason you taught for so many years? What would you say were your greatest educational accomplishments?

What if I asked your students to tell me what they thought seemed to matter most to you? I know it is not a lot of fun thinking about your own funeral, but it is one of the easiest ways to begin pondering your personal mission statement as a teacher and even as a person.

I must ask you some tough questions. Are you teaching in a way that corresponds to the answers of those questions? Are your interactions with students and colleagues helping you find fulfillment each day? When you plan lessons, do you do so with your main purposes of teaching in mind?

When you walk out of school each day, do you smile because you know you made a real difference in the lives of your students? Do you feel a sense of satisfaction and fulfillment as you recall the lessons you taught? Do former students call you, email you or stop by and see you to tell you how much of an impact you made in their lives? I imagine many of you can answer yes to those questions. Many of you cannot.

Until you identify the cornerstones of your life's foundation, you will never be able to align your values, gifts and mission with your teaching. Until that happens, you will always be less effective than you could be and find less joy in your career.

Regardless of how many lessons you plan or even how many of your students score well on an assessment, if your work with your students does not match your own mission, you will feel a sense of disillusionment after a while.

If you are like me, you occasionally get bogged down with the frustrating details of teaching and forget to remember the big picture. If you want a quick chuckle, remember the majority of staff meeting topics from the past year and think about how many of them were big picture issues.

Staff meeting topics normally include discussions of schedules, tardies, hallway monitoring, grading, discipline plans, testing, copy machine usage, dress codes, cell phone access, paperwork requirements, new programs, new curricula, evaluation procedures, etc. I smile just remembering those moments. These issues are important, but they tend to obscure the big picture.

Writing your personal mission statement lets you see the big picture again with clarity. Reviewing it often helps you deal with fire drills, dress code violations, seating charts, and intercom interruptions with perspective.

Toward the end of my career, I finally took the time to identify WHY I teach and WHAT it is I hope to accomplish in my time with students and colleagues. My personal mission statement has five parts and it is personal to me. Yours will not look like mine.

1 – To connect with my students and colleagues on a personal level and help them discover their strengths, gifts and passions as well as acknowledge their weaknesses.

2 – To develop my students' ability to think for themselves on a deeper, more critical level.

3 – To help my students understand science concepts and skills and help them to value the processes involved in scientific thinking and questioning.

4 – To lead with grace and try to reflect the love of God every day.

5 – To make an effort to improve the quality of life in every student, colleague and parent I come into contact with at school or in the community and to be an encourager for all.

Now that I am stepping out of the classroom into this new career as an educational speaker and consultant, my new mission statement is:

To encourage educators and provide them with fresh ideas and tools that will produce more effective, influential and enjoyable teaching.

Notice that these are *not* SMART goals – specific, measurable, attainable, realistic and timely. Goals are different from mission statements. Goals are detailed and definite; mission statements are big picture, timeless visions. Goals are good too, but they tend to narrow our focus and take our eyes off the grand scheme.

We have all heard the phrase, "I can't see the forest for the trees." This describes much of modern education today. Our focus on percentages, scores, plans and the latest data trend keeps our eyes averted from the big picture. The forest is an amazing place.

My teacher mission statement guided me through the last decade of my professional career. Having clear purposes for my teaching changed my effectiveness as a teacher and my enjoyment in my career. Your own teaching career is filled with countless challenges, but you will be less frustrated and find more joy if you feel like you are fulfilling your purpose and accomplishing your mission each day.

Having a clear purpose for your teaching gives you a reason to get up in the morning. It gives you a hope for tomorrow and a motivation for today. Having a clear mission statement helps you determine what NOT to do sometimes too.

There are many ways to develop your personal mission and purpose as a teacher, but I am going to give you a simple guide based on a variety of excellent resources.[xii]

---

1 - Get a pencil or pen or open your computer if you would rather use it.

2 - Try to find a quiet place to think and work.

3 - Write out your answers to the questions that follow.

4 - Be honest. Nobody is going to read what you write.

5 - Take your time and enjoy the process.

After careful consideration, answer as many of the following questions as possible. Be specific in your answers:

1 - What kinds of activities or events have you enjoyed in the past or enjoy doing now? What moments make you smile?

2 - What are you doing when you feel the best about yourself?

3 - Who inspires you? What qualities do you admire in that person?

4 - What are your natural gifts, talents and skills?

5   - When do people ask you for help?

6   - What would you regret not fully doing or having in your life?

7   - When you are older, looking back over your life and considering your accomplishments, which will matter to you the most?

8   - What are your deepest values? (List two or three)

9   - What are some challenges or difficulties you have overcome? How did you do it?

10 - If you could speak to a large crowd, what would your message be and who would be in the crowd?

After writing those answers down, reflect on them for a few minutes. List all the action words you used. *Example: educate, accomplish, empower, encourage, improve, help, give, guide, inspire, build, solve, integrate, master, motivate, nurture, organize, produce, promote, travel, spread, share, satisfy, understand, teach, write, etc.*

Narrow that list down to three or less. If you can settle on ONE that seems to be the most important one for you, that's even better.

Next, list everything and everyone you believe you can help. *Examples: People, students, teachers, creatures, organizations, causes, groups, environment, the world, etc.*

Finally, consider words that describe traits you value and prioritize them according to how important they are to you as an educator. *Examples: Hard-working, caring, energetic, creative, problem-solver, decision-*

maker, friendly, positive, family-oriented, honest, intelligent, compassionate, spiritual, analytical, passionate, organized, etc.

Narrow that list down to three or fewer.

A good, simple mission statement has three parts:

1 – What do I want to DO?

2 – WHO do I want to help?

3 – How is my work valuable to me and to others? What is the end result? How does WHAT I DO bring VALUE to me and WHO I want to help?

Try to combine these words into as few statements or sentences as possible. Try to limit yourself to a handful or fewer. Notice that I had five parts to my teacher mission statement but only needed one sentence for my educational speaking/consulting mission statement.

My mission statements both incorporate the word 'encourage.' I can sense discouragement and believe I have a God-given gift and responsibility to encourage people. I have always been that way and hopefully always will be. When I encourage people, I feel a deep sense of purpose and fulfilment. What do you believe you have to offer your students or your world?

Your personal mission statement is yours and it certainly will not look like either of mine. However, you also might identify one or two gifts or values you possess that help define your work as an educator. If you need more examples, do an internet search for personal mission statements.

Write out your mission statement here; why do you teach?

_____

_____

_____

_____

_____

_____

_____

_____

_____

_____

_____

Congratulations! If you completed this you are probably already starting to feel a little more excitement. There is freshness to your professional life when you identify your purpose for it. You are probably discovering a sense of purpose and motivation that you may have never had before or one you may have lost. Of course, you should tweak your mission statement as you go through life, making changes to match your own personal changes.

Even if you stopped reading now, you are far ahead of the majority of teachers who will be dragging themselves into work tomorrow, wondering why they ever decided to become a teacher in the first place. But do not stop reading. This is just the tip of this iceberg. It is about to get more interesting and more fun.

Other References: Chapter Five

Bangayan, Samantha. "Two reasons you need a personal Mission statement." Yellow Brick Road, (2011). www.yellowbrickroad.com. Web. November 2012.

Covey, Stephen R. *Seven Habits of Highly Effective People.* Free Press, (1989). Print.

Handall, Randall, Ph.D. "The five-step plan for creating personal mission statements." Quintessential Careers. www.quintcareers.com. Web. December 2012.

Santoro, Janna. "The art of the personal mission statement." WorkAwesome, (2010).

Su, Tina. "Life on Purpose: Fifteen questions to discover your personal mission." Think Simple Now, (2007). www.thinksimplenow.com. Web. November 2012.

Chapter Six - Understanding Your Personality

"Personality characteristics of the teacher are the electricity that brings the parts to life and determines the quality and effectiveness of teaching."
Elliot Eisner

After considering your mission as a teacher, taking the time to study your personality type is another step in the right direction. There are hundreds of books that hold all sorts of information about the unique individual you are. I am not recommending any particular online personality survey or a specific system or book, but I do recommend that you find a simple one that can begin to paint a picture that shows how you tick.

Visit *http://www.humanmetrics.com/cgi-win/jtypes2.asp* and take a few minutes to learn about yourself as a person. It is worth it. If you are not near a computer, just continue reading. I have put together some helpful and practical information that relates personality types to educators.

Of course, no single inventory or survey can describe a human's personality perfectly. People's personalities are a result of thousands of experiences, genetic combinations and subconscious events.

Before we look into this with any depth, we must realize the limitations. However, there is a lot of helpful information to be gained here and teachers should consider this a pre-test of sorts.[xiii]

Before we can improve, we need to know what our natural strengths and weaknesses are. We need to know why some tasks are easy for us while others are more difficult. We need to know why certain situations at school are fun and why some are frustrating.

None of us are alike. We know that about our students but somewhere along the way we have forgotten that all teachers are different in many ways, too. Teachers are as different as the students they teach.

Too many teachers do not even know what their own talents really are! Teachers use screwdrivers to hammer nails and hammers to drive screws and then wonder why their jobs are frustrating. If I have no clue what tools I carry to the job site, I am bound to experience frustration when the day begins.

I have witnessed hundreds of teachers in action during my career. When I combine research on personality types with educators I have known, I can categorize four main different types of teachers. Obviously, there are not just four types of teachers and even more obvious is the reality that no single educator's personality fits neatly into any of my four categories. Still, most of the teachers and administrators I know fit one of the four following types:

1 – The Rule-Following, Organized Teacher: Her desk is always neat and her lessons are always planned. Her grade book is always updated and papers are always neatly stacked. This teacher keeps orderly files and cannot stand messy work areas. Seating charts, following the rules and to-do lists are important. Making sure students (and colleagues) follow the rules is high on her list.

Colleagues look to the organized teacher for information relating to schedules, procedures, lunch menus, and dates. However, the organized teacher can be bossy, especially during meetings. She thinks there is one way to do things and any new ideas or brainstorming sessions are a waste of time. The organized teacher likes the status quo, "We've always done it this way and it has been working, so why change it?"

Most middle school and high school teachers have this type of personality. Rule following comes naturally, and in their minds, to do well in school involves compliance. Many administrators are of this nature as well. Education and its focus on rules and order produce its own kind. <u>Rule following, organized teachers can be tremendous educators and they are important on a school staff.</u>

2 – The Energetic, Quick to Act Teacher: This teacher is constantly on the go and jumps from one new teaching moment to another. He works hard at everything and is often a cheerleader for the staff. He expects everyone to work as hard as he does, students and colleagues included. However, this teacher often speaks and acts before

he thinks, putting his foot in his mouth from time to time. He is assertive and can become opinionated over time.

Colleagues look to the energetic teacher for help getting things done. If this teacher supports a project, he makes sure it gets completed in some way. However, the energetic teacher can lack depth of thought and has difficulty seeing the big picture. "Let's go, let's get something done, we don't need to talk about it any longer," might frequently flow from this teacher's mouth.

Many physical education teachers and coaches have this type of personality and so do some administrators. <u>Energetic, quick-to-act teachers can be tremendous educators and they are important on a school staff.</u>

3 – The Caring, Emotional Teacher: Of course, all teachers care. But the caring/emotional teacher has an extra ability to connect with students and is quick to pick up on verbal and non-verbal signals. This teacher is often seen in the hallway, comforting students and taking care of sick ones.

Colleagues look to the caring teacher for insight into students and into staff issues. This teacher can sense frustration among colleagues and might be forced to speak her mind in support or protection for herself or others. Her teaching is based in, "What's best for kids?"

However, the caring teacher is driven so strongly by emotion that she is often uninterested in educational theory and thought. Kids trump theories. Feelings trump logic and there are times getting approval from colleagues interferes with her decision making. These teachers tend talk too much and at times are offended by colleagues who show little dedication to their teaching.

Most elementary teachers have this type of personality and middle school and high school teachers of this type can find themselves at odds with their colleagues. There aren't many administrators of this type, but when they are, they are usually in elementary schools. <u>Caring, emotional teachers can be tremendous educators and they are important on a school staff.</u>

4 – The Analytical, Visionary teacher. This teacher is constantly trying new things and seldom repeats lessons in the same way from year to year. Detailed lesson plans and rule following is less important than educational research and theoretical study. Teachable moments are fun for this teacher and following 'pointless' rules is frustrating. He sees the big picture and is a visionary, often challenging the status quo. He is always asking, "Is there a better way to accomplish this goal or teach this lesson?"

Colleagues look to the analytical teacher for wisdom and advice but seldom take it. This teacher can seem weird, aloof and arrogant to others and often withdraws from the staff when non-essential (in his mind) topics are discussed. There are not many analytical teachers in our schools today; contemporary school structure discourages visionary thinking. The ones who are in schools often force themselves into new professions due to their disenchantment and cynicism.

Unless an administrator of this type has a capable, organized assistant, his visionary thinking can make the day-to-day operation of a school difficult.   Analytical, visionary teachers can be tremendous educators and they are important on a school staff.

All teachers are combinations of these four types, but most of us tend to fit more neatly into one of the types. Which of the four best matches you, as a teacher?   Can you admit that your teaching personality includes both strengths and weaknesses?   If so, you have learned the single most important lesson of this chapter: Simply acknowledging your strengths and weaknesses instantly makes you a better teacher. But do not stop there.

If you are as dedicated as I think you are, from this point on you will grow and learn about yourself. You will start to reach into personality types other than your own and grab useful tools there when necessary.

The unorganized teacher will find ways to become organized. The rule follower will become more flexible. The energetic teacher will realize the need for the occasional deeper thought.   The visionary teacher will appreciate a quick decision or two. We can become more rounded, capable and effective educators. We will see ourselves more clearly in the mirror and at the same time admire the beauty in the people standing behind us.

Still, we will function most often in our natural personality and the more awareness we have of that personality, the quicker we start growing as an educator. We understand why certain things in life come easier to us and why others are more difficult and frustrating. It is only then we can begin to see how we annoy others with our personality's flaws.

Before we move on, please list a few of the strengths and weaknesses of your personality here:

Strengths   Weaknesses

_____

_____

_____

_____

Of the weaknesses you listed, choose one you would like to improve on during the next few weeks. Do some reading, talk to your friends and colleagues and get some tips that will help you smooth out that particular rough edge in your life.

Finally, start being more comfortable with yourself. Enjoy the process of discovering who you are. We all have our personality quirks and we might as well be brave enough to admit them openly. One of your greatest accomplishments as a teacher and a person is to become so honest and sure of yourself that you can look in the mirror and laugh.

Most importantly, be who you are and what you are. This is the first step toward becoming better than you are. Outstanding teachers have a confidence to be themselves with their kids.

As I mentioned earlier, our students are not dumb; they pick up on any vibe we give. We need to be really relaxed. Walk into the room of an exceptional teacher and you will sense that relaxed atmosphere. The atmosphere in the magic kingdom is just different.

Other References: Chapter Six

"Jung Typology Test." Human Metrics. www.humanmetrics.com/cgi-win/jtypes2.asp. Web. January 2012.

Tieger, Paul. "Take our free personalitytype.com assessment." PersonalityType.com. www.personalitytype.com/quiz. Web. January 2012.

Chapter Seven - Discovering Your Own Learning Style

"Every one of us has a learning style as unique as our fingerprints."
Gordon Dryden

Educators should know more about how human brains work and the variety of learning types that fill those brains. Too many educators assume all brains work the same way. When we look out across our classes of students, I doubt if we consider the vast differences in the brains inside all those heads.

Brain researchers would agree that educators need to understand the brain more clearly if they intend to more effectively teach their students. Yes, it is helpful for teachers to understand their students' learning styles, but in my opinion, it is more helpful for a teacher to understand his or her own learning style first.

Before I jump into this, let me give you a brief review of learning styles. According to years of research, there are three main learning styles: visual, auditory and kinesthetic. Some experts in learning styles include a fourth, reading/writing.[xiv]

Visual learners generally think in terms of images. They find maps, graphs, charts, and other visual learning tools to be extremely effective. They remember lessons best by seeing someone show them how to complete a task. Visual learners prefer seeing an idea or thought sketched out on paper. This is me.

I like to see ideas and skills when I learn them. If you show me how to wire an electrical outlet, I will learn that skill much quicker than if you just told me how.

Auditory learners are those who generally learn best by listening. They typically like to learn through lectures, discussions, and reading aloud. They remember best by hearing someone tell them how to do something or by hearing themselves read a description aloud. This is not me. If someone talks too long in their explanation, I become Charlie Brown and hear nothing but droning syllables.

Kinaesthetic learners are those who learn best through touching, feeling, and experiencing the concepts they are trying to learn. They remember best by being actively involved in a task. I learn this way fairly well, too. Although I learn best by 'seeing it,' I like to 'get my hands on it,' too.

While most of us are able to learn using any of these styles, most of us learn best when we use the style that is most natural to us. It makes sense that students learn best when they are taught in their personal learning styles. A girl, who needs to 'see' things when learning them, will not absorb them as quickly if her teacher only lectures.

A boy, who needs to get his hands-on things while learning, will not learn as quickly if his teacher uses mostly video clips in class.

Students who really enjoy lectures and learn best by hearing explanations and stories get frustrated in totally hands-on learning environments.

This matters to us, as educators, because of the equally true fact that most teachers tend to teach in the style from which they learn best themselves. If you think in pictures and images or sketch out diagrams when working on a project, you are probably a visual learner, and most often, a visual teacher.

You use a lot of visual aids, diagrams, maps and charts in class. You put together power point presentations and incorporate video clips frequently into your lessons. You say, "Please LOOK at me," frequently during the day.

If you are someone who tends to think in sounds and language, would rather talk with people on the phone, and would rather get verbal directions, then you prefer to learn and teach in auditory ways. You enjoy lecturing, you have students read aloud in class and you say things like, "Please LISTEN to me."

Finally, if you get bored quickly in environments that are still and quiet and if you find yourself jumping right into a project without reading the directions, you lean toward kinesthetic learning. Kinesthetic learners ask to go to the restroom during classes just to get up and move around and take a break.

As teachers, you encourage active participation and often teach physical education, technology and skill-based classes. You say things like, "Please GET BUSY and GET SOMETHING DONE."

The most effective and powerful educators incorporate all three learning styles in their lessons. This is very difficult to do on a consistent basis. However, until an educator identifies her preferred learning style and begins to evaluate how often that style shows up in her teaching, she will not be as effective with all students as she can be. Let me give you a fictional example.

Mrs. Hughes (not a real person) has taught high school biology for many years. She runs a quiet ship and is very well respected throughout the community. She seldom has classroom management issues and is known as a teacher with high expectations.

Mrs. Hughes lectures every day and truly enjoys her subject area. She is extremely articulate and full of knowledge but she never uses visual aids or has her students do lab work.

Many of her students (auditory learners) learn an incredible amount in her class and some of those say that Mrs. Hughes is their favorite teacher. However, there are several other students who dread going to her class.

They fall asleep in class and ask to leave to the restroom as often as possible. Some end up failing her class and have to retake the course with another instructor. The students even blame themselves for failing.

Some students drop out of high school because of the failing grade in this class. Mrs. Hughes prides herself on her high standards and her reputation continues to spread.

True stories of this nature are told in thousands of schools across the country. Of course, one of the responsibilities of students and teachers is to adapt to styles of each other.

However, there is no reason educators cannot add a few simple strategies in order to better reach all types of learners.

Considering that kinesthetic learners are often forgotten in middle and high school classrooms, it would be a good idea to occasionally find ways to incorporate projects, debates, role playing, and other active forms of learning.

What is your most natural learning style; visual, auditory, or kinesthetic? Imagine someone records one of your classes and makes a television show using the footage. When you watch the recording, you study how much of your teaching seems to be visual, how much is auditory and how much promotes the kinesthetic learning style. Which of these three main learning styles is the one you use the least in your teaching now?

What could you do to add at least one strategy or activity from that style? Try that. You will not be sorry and your students will appreciate it.

Other References: Chapter Seven

Carbo, Marie, Dunn Rita, Dunn, Kenneth. *Teaching Students to Read Through Their Individual Learning Styles*. Pearson, (1986). Print. February 2012.

Haynes, Judie. *"Teach to Students' Learning Styles."* EverythingESL.net. www.everythingesl.net. Web. March 2012.

"Learning Styles for Teachers." About.com. www.712educators.about.com. Web. March 2012.

Chapter Eight: Connecting with Your Students

"We cannot teach students well if we do not know them well."
Hoffman and Leak

After spending decades in the classroom, reading countless books and articles on educational research, and observing teachers and students, there is one fact I know for sure.

Teachers who build positive relationships with their students and who take the time to connect with them in meaningful ways have found the key that opens the door to influential teaching. This chapter is so important it could be an entire book in itself.

Each year the students who enter our classrooms come from unique backgrounds, home situations, personal experiences and special challenges. They sit down at their desks with their gifts, talents, weaknesses and struggles and our job is to reach each one of them and help them learn.

In her book, *More Life through Management*, Alice Terry states, "A fundamental question for a student is, 'Does my teacher like me?'

Given a rigorous, aligned curriculum, the answer to that simple question is our best predictor of student achievement."[xv]

According to Dr. Robert Marzano and Dr. Debra Pickering in their book, *Dimensions of Learning*, "Today, we know more about teaching than we ever have before."

Research has shown us that teachers' actions in their classrooms have twice the impact on student achievement as do school policies regarding curriculum, assessment, staff collegiality, and community involvement.

The quality of the teacher-student relationship is the keystone for all other aspects of classroom management."[xvi] When a student misbehaves in an effective teacher's classroom, the teacher wants the behavior to stop and not happen again. The effective teacher wants prevention. When a student misbehaves in an ineffective teacher's room, that teacher often wants revenge and administers punishment.

Ineffective teachers send students to the office and expect the offender to be punished in some way. The teacher wants the student to be mad or hurt when he leaves the office. Punishment overrides true discipline. When a student is angry or hurt, what is a common response?

"Hurt people hurt people," states Will Bowen in his book, *Complaint Free Relationships: Transforming Your Life One Relationship at a Time*.[xvii] The student will probably not hurt the teacher because the teacher is an authority figure. So, who do you think becomes the target?

Educators speak about the need to stop bullying. Ironically, the biggest bullies in the school are often the teachers. A positive and respectful relationship between the teacher and his students is the cornerstone to learning. Both parties are responsible for the development of that relationship.

This is important stuff. Student achievement and classroom management are two crucial pieces of the educational puzzle. Not surprisingly, the two are closely related.

Show me a teacher who has classroom management issues and I will show you a classroom where students are not learning as much as they could. I know that from personal experience.

Early in my teaching career, when my classroom management skills were still a work in progress, my teaching was merely adequate at best. But as I began to understand the importance of building connections with all my students, my classroom management skills also began to improve, which in turn led to more effective teaching and greater student achievement.

Educational research shows that a well-managed classroom is one of the most important keys to effective teaching.[xviii]

When students feel connected or 'attached' to a teacher or to a school, two important things happen: they behave better and they learn better. The effects of this connection tend to be stronger for high-risk students.

In this day and age of increased accountability, the importance of teacher-student relationships is fundamental to the teaching/learning process. My own emphasis on this is seen in the first sentence of my teacher mission statement.

"To connect with my students and colleagues on a personal level and help

them discover their strengths, gifts and passions as well as acknowledge their weaknesses."

How do I know this is important? There are several pieces of evidence that tell me I'm headed in the right direction.

— *Although results on standardized tests are not the most important measure of teacher effectiveness, my students score well on science assessments. Ninety-six percent of them (127 out of 132) scored at 'meets standard' or above on the 2011 Kansas State Science Assessment.*

— *Parents tell me that they have to schedule their son or daughter's orthodontist appointments around my class.*

— *Students write me notes describing how I have impacted their lives.*

— *I have very few classroom management issues.*

— *Many of the high-risk students in my school find ways to stop in my room and talk, either before school, after school or during planning periods.*

— *Former students ask me to write reference letters.*

— *I get graduation and wedding invitations from former students.*

— *People call me at home, wondering if I could talk with a student or former student in crisis until professional help can be arranged.*

— *Students and former students have called me in the middle of the night when a parent has died unexpectedly. "I don't know who else to turn to and I know you care."*

Many of you experience the same kinds of events. Moments like that are evidence you are growing as an educator and that you have impacted your students forever.

The United States has spent several decades and several billion dollars on educational reform and where has it gotten us? Nation at Risk, Goals 2000, No Child Left Behind, and who knows what the next reform will be? We spend our time and our money focusing on statistics, test scores, curriculum, technology and goals.

Those things are important. Schools spend thousands of dollars on teacher training programs that focus on the latest and greatest educational fads, many which are ineffective or lack a research base.

When will our leaders realize we could change the face of education in this country by helping teachers learn to simply value each student and the background he or she brings to school each day? We would revolutionize education if teachers made greater efforts to simply listen to their students as much as we talk to them.

I started listening to my students more often. I started asking them questions about school and my own classroom. I am sharing a few of their responses here. Before you get all freaked out, I know these are middle school students and I know they do not have a lot of life experience. I know they often do not know what is best for them.

But still, read these comments some of my students made in regard to a question I posed about how much real thinking schools actually require and what their opinion of school was, in general.

13-year-old female student – *"There is life, then there is school. The two never mix during school."*

14-year-old male student – *"So much of school is just pointless. I can get A's without ever having to think or really learn anything. I get so bored because it's* the same routine over and over and either I already know what we're studying or it is obviously irrelevant to life. I have a lot of things I'd like to learn about, but I'm stuck there with the rest of the class."

13-year-old male student – "I have noticed that the teaching profession attracts bossy people. It's more important that they show they are in control than they are really listening to us or teaching. Just about everything in school seems pointless to me. And you never want to have your own idea about how to do something; well, I can see why that is, because if the students had any thoughts about the lesson, it would throw off the teachers' lesson plans and then things would get out of control."

13-year-old male student – "I love to learn stuff on my own. We have those computer carts and I'd love to go get a laptop, get on the online textbook and go. I bet right now no one is using the laptops in this building. But we have to stay with the group, reviewing things over and over, even when I already learned them the first time."

14-year-old male student – "I get home; I'm already tired, and school is really busy for me. I'm in band and football; I try to be interested in class and do my work. I don't really have any seminar time. When I get home, I have lots of chores to do; mainly, I have to do all the laundry for my family. Most nights I have to fold every piece of laundry just right or I get in trouble. Then, I eat something and try to do my homework, which on a lot of nights takes about an hour. If it is a game night or some other school activity night, I might be up after midnight getting everything done. I'm so tired in the morning."

13-year-old male student – "I'm a kinesthetic learner; I have to be able to move around. If I sit too long, I can't make it. I make up an excuse, like I need to go to the restroom or get a drink, just to get up and go walk around. I bet no one who asks to go to the bathroom really goes. They are just so bored or tired they have to get up and take a break. (*Everyone in the class agreed.*) If teachers just let us move around a little bit or let us get up to take a break once each class it would be better. But I'd still like to be doing something with my hands more often."

13-*year-old female student* – "I've learned how to look interested in class. I stare ahead, take notes, and stay awake; but, I usually have no idea of what is going on in class. I'm not a very good note-taker so I just write down things word for word, but I never know what I'm writing. And I never look at the notes again."

14-*year-old male student* – "I've noticed that by the end of the day, all the teachers are grouchy. They must be really tired or their patience is gone or something. I really don't like it when teachers get upset with one class and then it spills over into their other classes. But I've really noticed that this year, teachers are tired or something during their last classes."

13-*year-old male student* – "I know a lot of us are wondering why we have this extra math to do when it wasn't our class that did poorly on the assessments. Our class has always tested well, but we are being punished for the 9th graders and their problems. Now we have math every day; we have MTSS every day and we have lots of math homework every night."

13-*year-old male student* – "I think it's funny when teachers try to tell us how much we will use what we are studying in real life. They try, they really do, but we know. Like the math problem about painting a fence. If you are painting at a certain rate with one kind of a brush and your friend is painting at a certain rate with another, how long will it take you to paint the fence? Just paint the fence already! There are too many variables that would affect this."

13-*year-old female student* – "It seems like there are only two answers at school - something is either right or it is wrong. What about the middle area? What about the times when there is a lot that might affect if something is right or *wrong? I think one of the reasons why we don't think much is because it is easier for teachers to have a right or wrong answer and real thinking sometimes isn't like that. It's easier to grade, I guess."*

14-year-old male student — "I think it would be cool if school had a class or a time when we could sit and think and talk about things that really mattered."

13-year-old male student — "I know I'm kind of a 'bad' kid, but I feel like some teachers watch me and wait until I do something wrong, then they jump all over me."

12-year-old female student — "The one thing that frustrates me about teachers is that they 'pretend' to listen. I can tell when a teacher is really listening because when they aren't, their eyes glaze over and have a dullness to them. I've seen it for years. They can't fool us. We all know."

12-year-old male student — "I've been in math class and I already know everything we have been doing. I'm so bored but I am stuck there. For some reason once you are put in a math level you can't get out."

Even if you take those comments with a grain of salt and acknowledge that these students are only in middle school, you are blind if you cannot see some truth in them. Their words and thoughts forced me to take a long look into my teacher mirror.

The more I ponder my interactions with my students over the years and the more I study the teaching/learning process, the more frustrated I become with much of our current teaching culture.

Throughout the history of public education in America, one of the main goals has been to produce compliant, robotic learners who will be able to move out into the workforce and become compliant, robotic employees. The relationship between teacher and student is often business-like and missing any human warmth.

Knowing that many teachers have reservations about connecting with their students, I would like to offer a couple of reassuring steps to get started along the way.

The first step in establishing influential and appropriate relationships with students is the teacher's ability to provide clear and strong expectations and guidance in academic and behavioral areas.

In a study (Chiu & Tulley, 1997) that involved interviews with more than 700 students in grades 4–7, students articulated a clear preference for strong teacher guidance and control rather than more permissive types of teacher behavior.[xix]

In hundreds of other studies, of all the variables involved in teaching, classroom management had the largest effect on student achievement. This is common sense; students cannot learn in a chaotic, poorly managed classroom.

There are many educators who shy away from connecting with students because they are afraid of becoming pushovers or 'buddies' in their students' eyes. Nothing is further from the truth.

Truly effective teachers are able to establish clear guidelines for behavior, hold high academic expectations and are still able find ways to connect with their students in real, powerful ways.

My own classroom management system was an adaptation of an idea I stole and tweaked from one of Jim Fay's *Love and Logic* conferences I attended in Wichita about fifteen years ago.[xx]

On the first day of class each year, I had every student get out a sheet of paper and draw a horizontal line across the middle of it. I called the activity, 'Drawing the Line.' I asked the students to give me words that described ways people SHOULD treat each other when they are in a social setting.

Words such as kind, helpful, respectful, honest, etc. came from the students and were added to the top half of the sheets of paper. I added these words on the board while the students did the same on their papers. I tried to encourage the students to think of any type of positive behavior. Usually a class, with some prompting, came up with fifteen or more words.

At this point, I had the students come up with the opposites of each word. They produced some acceptable work pairs: kind-mean, helpful-selfish, respectful-rude, honest-cheating, etc. We put the opposite behaviors on the bottom half of the paper; leaving a small space open at the very bottom for later.

'Below the line behavior' would include rude comments from either the teacher or the students, inappropriate language from either, pushing or shoving, expressions of boredom or disinterest, sarcastic putdowns, etc.

We all know what that kind of behavior looks like, even when teachers exhibit it.

I told the students that our class would be an 'above the line,' class. We would all treat each other in 'above the line' ways. I treated them in those ways, they treated me in those ways and they treated each other in those ways too.

Instantly and secretly, I had already started connecting with my students. When they saw me following the same guidelines for my behavior toward them as they are expected to show toward me and others, a common bond was begun. Students had immediate 'say' or autonomy in our classroom.

Eventually someone asked, "What happens if one of us goes below the line?" If they didn't ask, I prompted the question. When someone (remember, it could be me) treated anyone else in this room in a 'below the line' way, he or she was expected to fix things immediately and deal with the appropriate consequences respectfully. We had to talk about how we fix things in life: apologies, changed attitudes, picking up the spit wad and throwing it away, refraining from talking, etc.

If the offender couldn't fix the problem on his or her own or couldn't face the necessary consequences of poor behavior, 'something else' was going to happen and I fixed the problem for them.

Although I was under the same 'above the line' system as my students were, I was still the authority and had the ability and responsibility to enforce poor behavior with appropriate consequences. The 'something else' gave me a lot of flexibility and let me deal with each issue in a personal way.

For some students, a consequence of 'below the line' behavior was a stern glance or a small shaking of my head. Others needed a new seat or a talk in the hall. Still others required a parent call or a detention. However, for me, nearly all problems were fixed by the students with little enforcement needed from me.

Students were quick to pick up on this system and told each other (and me), "That was below the line." In fact, I still hear those words from students I had over ten years ago when I run into them at games or Wal-Mart. The most important part of this system was that the line is clearly drawn, understood and enforced.

My daughter, Amber, uses her own model of this system in her middle school classroom. She told me that her students stand up and agree on each behavior before it is included on the class chart. I like that and wish I would have done that too.

A few of my colleagues over the years thought I was too 'easy' on my students. Nothing is further from the truth. Both my students and I were consistently holding the 'line' in front of each other every day. There were immediate and constant adjustments made, apologies given and consequences shared. Positive classroom behavior was a secret part of every lesson plan and activity.

Of course, there will always be more serious behavior issues that come up from time to time. Even the best teachers have to deal with the occasional serious discipline case. I still had to call parents; I gave a handful of detentions each year and, in extreme cases, still removed a student from my class for a day or more.

Still, the number of those types of more chronic or serious issues decreased dramatically once I started using the 'Above the Line' classroom management system. I started having more fun and so did the students. We all learned much more along the way.

At the very bottom of the paper, in the space I said to leave open earlier, I wrote two large words, DANGEROUS and ILLEGAL. I told the class that this area represented 'Bottom Line Behavior,' which I did not let them fix.

If a student did something dangerous or broke the law in my classroom, he or she was sent to the office immediately - no comments, questions, or explanations allowed. In these cases, I wanted the administrators and/or police officers involved.

These dangerous or illegal situations were the only times I sent a student to the office in my last few years of teaching. I handled all other behavior issues.

However, if a student pulled a chair out from under another student, threw a book across the room, or started a fight, the offender(s) was directed to the office. A quick phone call to the office, BRIEFLY explaining the incident is always a good idea then too.

If the student refused to go to the office, I called the office back and informed the administrators of the situation and if necessary, our school resource officer intervened. This actually happened once. I removed the remaining students and took them to the library while our SRO handled the situation.

My classroom was a safe place and the students knew it. It was safe emotionally, intellectually and physically. In the course of every school year, there were two or three cases I considered 'dangerous' enough for the student to be sent to the office.

Fortunately, I can only remember two or three cases in the past decade when 'illegal' fit the situation. I am sure there are many of you who face that type of behavior several times each month. I am also sure that many of you never face that type of behavior.

Each school is different and each one has its own unique virtues and challenges. Each one is full of dedicated educators who have learned how to make a difference in the lives of the young people they try to reach and teach.

In review, the first step in making influential connections with students is to develop clear guidelines for academic rigor and appropriate behavior and consistently enforce them with appropriate consequences.

Second, once you lay the groundwork for how your classroom will operate, you are now ready to start taking a personal interest in your students. The goal is not to become friends; the goal is to establish a connection between two people who have learning in common. I have never known a student who did not appreciate personal attention from a teacher.

Finding the time to give this kind of attention to each of your students is very difficult if you teach in a middle or high school setting. But it is possible with a little effort and creativity.

If you are interested in connecting with your students, you must be intentional in doing so, it will not happen by chance. Here are a few ideas I have picked up over the years that have worked for me:

1 - Spend several class periods early in the year focused on learning about your students' interests, strengths, and weaknesses.

2 - Show your students that you are a real person; admit you make mistakes and are still learning right along with them.

3 - Use show and tell moments. (This is not just for elementary school or students)

4 - Study personalities and learning styles and spend some time sharing what you discover with each other.

5 - Make early deposits in 'toughest' kids early. If you have put something into a student's life, there is something there to pull out from when discipline is required.

6- Notice things about your students: new hair, new glasses, getting taller, etc.

7- Catch your students doing good things and let them overhear you praising them among your colleagues or other students.

8 - Use appropriate touches when possible: handshakes, hand on shoulder, high fives, hugs, etc.

9 - Really listen to each student when he or she talks.

10- Discover hobbies, interests, etc.

11- Talk informally with students before, during, and after class.

12- Greet students outside of school; for instance, at games or at the store.

13 - Single out a few students each day in the hall and talk with them briefly.

14 - Be aware of and comment on important events in students' lives such as participation in sports, drama, or other extracurricular activities.

15 - Compliment students on important achievements in and outside of school.

16 - Meet students at the door as they come into class; greet each one by name whenever possible.

17 - Make eye contact with each student at least once each class period. Teachers can make eye contact by scanning the entire room as they speak and by freely moving about all sections of the room.

18 - Give credit for ideas to the students who come up with them.

19 - Allow and encourage all students to participate in class discussions and interactions.

20 - Make sure to call on students who do not commonly participate, not just on those who respond most frequently.

Teacher-student relationships build a solid foundation for effective classroom management. Effective classroom management is a key to high student achievement. Teacher-student relationships must be intentionally cultivated and not be left to chance.

By using strategies supported by research, teachers can influence the operation of their classrooms and build strong teacher-student relationships that will impact student learning in positive, lasting ways.

There are a few final thoughts on this important matter. In any average classroom across the country, there are students who struggle with mental, emotional or behavioral disorders.

Many of these students receive little or no services at school or home. A teacher who connects with each of his or her students, including those with high needs, often provides the one place where those students experience a positive learning environment and get their needs addressed.

Students living in poverty and other at-risk students face their own unique challenges. Influential teachers are even more important to poor and at-risk students. For a lot of students, school is the only safe place they know. School is an oasis, a place of stability and love.

Teachers give students consistency they often do not get at home. The students receive attention, respect and have the opportunity to learn things and grow. It is normal to see at-risk students making huge academic gains with an effective teacher.

This goes beyond culture and economic status. Powerful teaching is about looking at each child as an individual, not as a number. Differentiated instruction is the current buzzword but effective teachers have been 'differentiating' with their students forever. "How did the game go last night?" "How does your family celebrate birthdays?" "Write a story about a time you were afraid."

Exceptional teaching involves building a level of trust and openness in each student. Students must feel that they are protected and that someone really cares. Do students know if they have an fantastic teacher? Absolutely! Young people are not fooled. They look forward to coming to school. They want to interact. They want to be honored and valued for what they have to contribute. Youngsters blossom and grow.

Effective teachers connect with kids. They build a bridge between school and their parents, their homes, their communities and their world. Every single student brings hundreds of stories with them to school. Those stories are the framework for their lives and teachers must value and honor students' backgrounds, families, cultures and economic situations. It is not just the stories students *BRING TO* school; it is the stories that great teachers *PULL OUT* of them - their dreams, their hopes, their goals.

Outstanding teachers truly understand what makes their students tick. Paulo Frierre, in his amazing book, *Pedagogy of the Oppressed*, helped me understand this vital concept.[xxi]

Effective teachers can interact and connect with all types of students. They don't treat all students the same way and they have an ability to use different methods to connect with the different types of students they teach. Ineffective teachers do not have this ability and can be insensitive of the wide variety of needs of the students in their classrooms. It is clear that a teacher's ability to connect with all types of students is essential before powerful, influential teaching can occur.

Other References: Chapter Eight

Brophy, J. E. *Teaching Problem Students.* The Guilford Press. 1996. Print.

Brown, John. *Observing Dimensions of Learning in Classrooms and Schools.* Virginia: ASCD, 1995. Print.

Chiu, L. H. and Tulley, M. "Student preferences of teacher discipline styles." *Journal of Instructional Psychology, 1997.* 168-175. March 2012.

Fay, Jim. *Love & Logic.* Love and Logic Press, (1995). Print.

Freire, Paulo. *Pedagogy of the Oppressed.* New York: Bloomsbury Academic, 30th Anniversary Edition, 2000. Print.

Glasser, William. *Schools Without Failure.* New York: Perennial Library Harper & Row. First Edition, 1969. Print.

Glasser, William. *The Quality School: Managing Students Without Coercion.* New York: Harper Perennial, 1998. Print.

Kerman, S., Kimball, T., and Martin, M. *Teacher Expectations and Student Achievement.* Phi Delta Kappa International Inc., 1980. Print.

Marzano, Robert J., Daisy E. Pickering, and Jane Pollock. *Classroom Instruction That Works. Virginia: ASCD,* 2001. Print.

Marzano, R. J. *What Works in Schools*. Virginia: ASCD, 2003. Print.

Levy, Jack. *Do You Know What You Look Like? Interpersonal Relationships in Education*. Routledge, 1993. Print.

Terry, Alice. *More Life Through Management*. Creative Teaching Press. Print. 1998.

Chapter Nine – Filling Your Toolbox

"People who don't use the tools given to them only injure themselves."
Debra Wilson

I enjoy building things and attempting DIY projects. I have developed enough skill to be the family 'fix-it guy.' I finished our basement, built a cool garage/shed, and designed and constructed a four-level deck. I have completed countless electrical, tiling, painting and plumbing projects.

Here is what I learned from those ventures: tools make a difference when it comes to completing projects with quality. Better tools equal better work. A wider variety of tools allows a person to produce a better project.

I used to have one old hand saw, the kind you picture being used to painstakingly saw a branch off a tree. Now I have several different saws - some manual, some electric - and they all help me in different ways. As my toolbox filled up, the quality of my work increased dramatically as has the difficulty of the projects I tackle.

Effective, influential teachers do more than just transfer information to their students. Exceptional teachers spread a love of learning and are constantly learning, growing and adding more tools to their own teacher toolboxes. They do not just open their textbook and move through it robotically.

I am not opposed to textbooks; they are one of many useful tools. However, I do not agree with textbooks being at the heart of curriculum decisions. I am afraid that more often than not, it is the textbook that determines what is taught in schools today.

Exceptional teachers have several tools, each with a different purpose. There is an excitement and enthusiasm in their classrooms. There is a lot of thinking, questioning and wondering. Effective teachers are always finding fresh ideas.

They are eternal students. Howard Hendricks once said, "I would rather my students drink from a flowing stream than from a stagnant pond."[xxii] A teacher may start her career with only a few simple tools, but she will learn, grow and continue to add tools until her very last day with students, if she stays fresh.

This chapter is your flowing stream and there are going to be teacher tools floating by for you to take and use. Even if you only reach out and grab a couple to put in your own toolbox, you can expect those tools to push your teaching to the next level. Okay, get ready. The water is about to start flowing your way. Look for anything that seems to fit a need for you right now. The list is lengthy, but extremely practical.

I define these tools as tips, strategies, best practices, ideas, suggestions, and requirements. I encourage you to grab a highlighter and mark any that seem like a good match for your teaching style, your grade level and your curriculum. I must acknowledge my admiration of Harry Wong's, *The First Days of School*, at this point. Several of his ideas appear here.[xxiii]

1 - Welcome students to class; catch them in the hall as they enter, if possible.

2 - Make students realize your class will be different. The first ten minutes of the first day is crucial. Whatever you do, don't just read through the class roster, mispronouncing names and passing out textbooks like the first day is drudgery that must be survived. Tell a story, sing a song, read a book, produce a video about your class - anything other than the normal first day monotony.

3 - Make students know they will learn a lot and have success in your class.

4 - Take time to make sure students know you are going to care about them and that you are here to teach THEM a subject, not to teach a SUBJECT to them.

5 - Expose yourself a bit; let students start to understand the person in you.

6 - Use name tags, tents - anything that will let you use their names right away.

7 - Use journal/log entries as warm-ups. Stretch their minds each day, maybe even the very first day.

8 - Teach and practice purposes, guidelines, routines, and procedures early and often.

9 - Find a management system that works for you but use your personality, be yourself! Let the students have some input into how the classroom will operate. A sense of autonomy is a strong motivator for anyone.

10 – Hope for problems, expect trouble; look who you are dealing with!

11 – Never force behavior and avoid power struggles; many students have seen more abuse than you could ever possibly give and the more you force, the more you will lose.

12 – Let respect grow on its own – some students don't know what respect looks like; you have to show respect to them first. You will have to teach them about common social behavior.

13 – Make early deposits; especially with class leaders, at-risk students, and 'rowdies.'

14 – Find a grading system that works for you and impacts all students, but say often, "It is not just about a grade!"

15 – Smile more.

16 – Read *The Shrinking of Treehorn*[xxii], *The Sneetches*[xxv], or *The Rainbow Fish*[xxvi]. Use picture books for all ages and take the time to talk about their meaning. There are picture books that relate to most subject areas and concepts; it just takes a little effort to find them.

17 – Make your room easy to rearrange; make the room match the activity.

18 – Building relationships with students is the KEY to effective teaching!

19 – Notice something special about your students; catch them in the hall, before, during, or after class, talk about their big play in the game, their new hair style, how you saw them doing something cool. When you are with a student, be there with him!

20 – Do not send homework unless you have a real reason for it. To have something to base a grade on is not good enough. If you give homework just to have grades in the grade book, please reevaluate your homework. What do your grades measure?

21 – Time activities, keep a clock and stick to it most of the time. Shift gears frequently. Students of all ages need brain breaks; the younger the student, the more frequent the breaks.

22 – Always extend your questioning so deeper thinkers are drawn into discussions. Wait a few seconds after asking deeper questions; longer wait time equals deeper thinking.

23 – Have a seating chart for at least the first few days so everyone knows where to sit. If you want to operate without seating charts, wait until later in the year.

24 – Study each class carefully; they will all have their own unique atmospheres. What works for one class may not work for others. Be ready to adjust your teaching based on the class.

25 – Dress professionally, have your room orderly, have flawless hygiene and be on time.

26 - Be a life-long learner.

27 – Create a positive atmosphere in your classroom.

28 – Be flexible; there is bound to be a fire drill when you least

expect it or want it.

29 – Have a sense of humor. Tell a cheesy joke on occasion.

30 – Get to know your students and let your students get to know you on some level.

31 – Establish clear expectations for classroom behavior and academic work.

32 – Admit your mistakes and limitations often.

33 – Teach in a way that reaches all learning styles.

34 - Be consistent but address each situation on a personal level.

35 – Vary class routines occasionally.

36 – Break long instructional periods down into smaller segments with some type of break between each.

37 – Read picture books, tell stories, show video clips, use role playing, etc.

38 – Do not be bound by the textbook.

39 – Show how what you are teaching is applicable in life. Encourage students to ask, "Why are we learning this?" If you cannot answer that question, you should do some research before continuing.

40 – Write a little each day; journal, logs, stories, etc.

41 – Keep up with technology and ask students for help with it.

42 – Consider using new ways of assessing learning.

43 – Brag about your colleagues in front of your students.

44 – Brag about your students in front of your colleagues.

45 – Invite your administrator into your classroom when you

are doing something cool. Brag about your students in front of him or her. Brag about your administrator in front of your students.

46 – Take a lot of pictures during class activities and post them in the room and in the halls.

47 – Read Marcia Tate's book, *Worksheets Don't Grow Dendrites*, and start to incorporate a few of her strategies I've listed here:[xxvii]

Brainstorming and discussion

Drawing and artwork

Field trips

Games

Graphic organizers, semantic maps and word webs

Humor

Manipulatives, experiments, labs and models

Metaphors, analogies and similes

Mnemonic devices

Movement

Music, rhythm and rap

Project-based and problem-based

instruction

Reciprocal teaching and cooperative- learning

Role plays, drama, pantomimes, charades

Storytelling

Technology

Visualization and guided imagery

Visuals

Work study and apprenticeships

Writing and journals

48 – Read Harry Wong's book, *The First Days of School* and steal a few of his ideas.[xxviii]

49 – Read Todd Whitaker's book, *What Great Teachers Do Differently* and try some of his stuff.[xxix]

50 - Ignore minor disturbances and handle behavior issues without making them worse.

51 - Be quick to apologize when you are at fault.

52 - Never talk negatively about a colleague or another student in front of your class.

53 – Do not play favorites.

54 - Keep your administrator aware of any potential parent issues.

55 - Give options on assignments whenever possible.

56 - Know your standards/indicators and learn math and reading standards, too.

57 - Roughly plan out your entire year, aligning that plan with the required curriculum and standards.

58 - Use a lesson plan format that works for you.

59 - Read and understand low-income/poverty students' unique challenges. Ruby Payne's, *Understanding Poverty*, is excellent.[xxx]

60 - Support your administrators – Be enthusiastic about your school. Make them notice.

61 - Change starts with one person. You can be the difference

in your school!

Other References: Chapter Nine

Hendricks, Howard. *Teaching to Change Lives: Seven Proven Ways to Make Your Teaching Come Alive.* Colorado Springs, Colorado: Multnomah Books, 1998. Print.

Payne, Ruby. *Framework for Understanding Poverty.* Highlands, Texas: Aha Process Inc., Fourth Edition, 2005. Print.

Tate, Marcia. *Worksheets Don't Grow Dendrites.* Thousand Oaks, California: Corwin, Second Edition, 2010. Print.

Whitaker, Todd. *What Great Teachers Do Differently.* Eye on Education, 2003. Print.

Wong, Harry. *The First Days of School.* Mountain View, California: Harry K. Wong's Publications. 2004. Print.

Chapter Ten: Defining Learning

"I want to talk about learning, but not the lifeless, sterile, futile, quickly forgotten stuff that is crammed in to the mind of the poor helpless individual tied into his seat by ironclad bonds of conformity! I am talking about LEARNING - the insatiable curiosity that drives the adolescent boy to absorb everything he can see or hear or read about gasoline engines in order to improve the efficiency and speed of his 'cruiser'. I am talking about the student who says, "I am discovering, drawing in from the outside, and making that which is drawn in a real part of me." I am talking about any learning in which the experience of the learner progresses along this line: "No, no, that's not what I want"; "Wait! This is closer to what I am interested in, what I need"; "Ah, here it is! Now I'm grasping and comprehending what I need and what I want to know!"

Carl Rogers

Everybody is talking about education. Politicians, media outlets, teachers, parents, business leaders, and students are all spouting out opinions and criticisms of education today. Sadly, few of them actually understand what learning means and involves. Without a foundational grasp of the teaching/learning process, the answer most seem to have to the question about educational improvement is to throw more money, new programs, increased standards and updated curricula at schools and measure learning by adding more assessments. Little in-depth thought about the nature of learning occurs.

What ends up passing for education often ends up hurting our youth more than helping them. We produce better test takers who cannot fix leaky faucets, balance their bank accounts, listen to their neighbors or reflect on their own lives. Today's students also realize that much of their learning seems pointless.

Research and theories about the nature of learning could fill several library shelves. But studying research and theories is hard mental work and people involved in education often don't have the time, desire or energy required. It seems ironic that educators seldom dive deeply into the subject of thinking and learning.

You would think that of all career professions, educators would be the last to settle for the quick fix or the Band-Aid approach to school improvement. You would think that educators would be most interested in how the brain works and what is necessary for long-term retention. My hope is that by sharing a few thoughts about the nature of learning, some who read this will be challenged to pursue a greater understanding of learning on their own.

In my psychology class at Bethany College in the fall of 1975, learning was probably defined as new knowledge or a new skill that resulted in a change of behavior. That definition is still widely used and accepted. According to that traditional definition, the process of learning results in a noticeable change of some type.

A basketball player learns how to shoot a proper left-handed layup and the assessment of his learning will show up in the next drill or game situation. But, does a student have to 'show something' to demonstrate learning has happened? New brain research is shedding new light on the subject of learning, what it is and how it best occurs.

The latest research has found that learning should be seen as being a process rather than a momentary spewing of facts and information. Learning does not always have to 'show up' right away in some act or assessment score. Some learning plants seeds or builds a foundation for future lessons. Learning can also build mental muscle that will not be used in a practical sense until years later. Other learning is reflective in nature and in that way is a personal and somewhat secret gift no one else would even notice.[xxxi]

Motivation plays a huge part in learning as well. Learning can happen with or without any conscious awareness. Many experts have evidence that humans might begin learning long before birth.[xxxii]

Without any understanding of education, babies learn hundreds of skills and interpersonal behaviors in their first year.

The depth of learning that occurs during the more formal teaching/learning process also depends on the nature of the activity and the effectiveness of the teacher. Teachers who understand the thinking and learning process are obviously better able to push students into deeper thinking and learning.

Bloom's taxonomy helps educators understand the differing depths of learning, but Bloom merely pulled back the shades to the window of thought.

The latest revised version of Bloom's taxonomy is easy to grasp, but difficult to incorporate into the classroom.[xxxiii] [xxxiv] However, it is essential that all teachers, from pre-school teachers through university graduate professors, teach in ways that produce all of the types of learning and thinking found in the familiar triangular graphic.[xxxv]

I agree with some current researchers who say that Bloom's triangle should not always be seen as a progressive tool.[xxxvi] For example, it is not necessary to begin at the memorizing and factual level with every learning activity. These levels are interchangeable and the entire triangle can be turned upside down at times.

I often like to start teaching concepts at the evaluating stage and then working my way up or down from there. A kindergarten student can evaluate more than we are aware. Imagine a scene at lunch where a kindergarten boy tells his teacher, "I like chocolate milk better than white milk." The teacher asks, "Why do you like chocolate better?" With his answer, whatever it is, the 5-year-old gets to exercise his mind.

Without asking why, an opportunity for thinking is lost. Influential and effective teachers (and parents) take their youngsters into the deeper recesses of the mind all the time. As a commercial once said, "The mind is a terrible thing to waste."[xxxvii] I agree.

Kindergarten students are capable of all of these levels of thought. The key is in the teacher's recognition of her students' awareness and the types of questions she asks. Young children can analyze, evaluate and create as well as anyone, relative to their ages.

Teachers of all ages must develop the ability to question, guide and prompt students so they explore all levels.

Young people love to think. If you do not believe me, start asking your children and grandchildren deeper questions. Practice your questioning skills. Let those young brains do what they are made to do. Be ready to smile and be amazed. There is one word of caution here.

Once your students begin really using their minds, they will find the common worksheet experience dull and lifeless. They will expect to enjoy using their minds when they walk into your room.

Throughout the years, teachers have spent most of their time in the 'remembering' level. Students learn factual knowledge, memorize it, regurgitate it for a test and then often forget it. When students make real sense of a concept and begin to see it abstractly, the sky is the limit. As I will touch on later, simple compare/contrast activities are great at any level. Metaphors and analogies should be used as often as possible.

The deeper a classroom of students and teacher dives into real thought, the more enjoyable the process is for all involved. Helping students interpret knowledge and begin to understand it in different ways is exciting and fun.

Helping them learn how to form opinions, challenge positions, debate, and present alternatives, is exhilarating. Helping them see inside themselves, make improvements and set out to make a difference in the world is magical.

One final look at Bloom's taxonomy is necessary. The lower the stage of learning, the more external the learning is. But as students begin to apply and analyze what they learn, the learning becomes more and more internal.

The difference is like learning how babies are made in a sixth-grade puberty lesson compared to holding your sick baby daughter in your arms all night and realizing that you would sacrifice yourself for her.

It is like memorizing the symptoms of Alzheimer's disease compared to holding your father's hand as you lead him around the hospital in his final days of battling the disease. It is the teacher's job (and joy) to find some strategy or technique to promote deep diving as often as possible.

The teaching/learning process is more effective when the learner:

- has some previous understanding of the concept.

- has a personal connection to the concept.

- is developmentally ready to grasp the concept.

- sees a purpose or reason for learning the concept.

Learning can be forced on someone, but the depth of the learning is limited in that case.

Do people always know when they are learning? Are students aware they are engaged in the learning process? The answers are interesting.

Formal education occurs whenever people come together in an organized and structured manner for the purposes of learning.[xxxviii] Schools, teacher in-services, driver's education, professional development days, training sessions, conferences, Alcoholics Anonymous meetings, *How to Tile a Floor* classes at Home Depot, etc., are all times and places for formal learning. People realize they are supposed to learn something at these events. They expect to learn and have learning on their minds. Someone plans the learning.

Although formal learners are in a structured learning environment, they must still often be motivated to learn. Extrinsic and intrinsic rewards are used with varying degrees of success. Teachers have a thousand ways to motivate their students. The ability to motivate people is a skill that should be developed through professional development events.

A good way to motivate students is by creating a classroom environment that embraces learning and gives great value and joy to the stretching of the brain. Learning is the heart of classroom activities, not grades or busy work. The teacher in this type of environment is quick to admit mistakes and often asks students for help. I made a poster with the following words and mounted it in the hall at the entrance to my classroom.

Think for yourself.
The teacher in this room may be wrong.

We live in an increasingly gullible and naïve society, one filled with con-artists and scams. Without the ability to think critically, analyze sources, and discern truth and fiction, people put themselves in danger. This discernment doesn't come naturally; it must be cultivated and practiced.

Another crucial motivational tool is the connection that is made between teacher and student. The stronger the connection, the more students are motivated to learn from that teacher.

Informal education can happen anytime.[xxxix] Without realizing it, we learn life lessons outside of structured settings all the time. The toilet quits working, the car will not start, the baby has a bad cough and taxes are due.

Life happens and we have to learn on the fly to survive. We seldom realize we are learning in the midst of those storms. This kind of learning often settles more deeply than formally learned concepts. We all know how mistakes are often our best teachers.

I certainly was not intending to learn anything when I failed at my first attempt at kissing. But I did.

I learned you should never poke your girlfriend in the eye with the collar of your letter jacket when you move in to kiss her for the first time. If you do, she will laugh at you and you will feel miserable for a long time.

I learned that you have to pick yourself up and try again. I learned you can recover from a disastrous first kiss. That girl who crushed my dreams of a perfect first kiss has been my wife now for the past 35 years.

Informal learning usually has its own motivational factor. People have to use the toilet (so the toilet must be fixed), they have to travel to work (the car has to start), the baby needs to feel better (everyone has to sleep) and jail awaits a non-taxpaying citizen. Is it not interesting that memorable learning happens without any structure and without any additional motivation required? Can schools learn something from this?

Both types of learning can happen at school, but the teacher cannot just teach his planned lessons, he must also be on the lookout for the teachable moments. I like to call those kinds of teaching moments, 'chasing the rabbit.' More and more, teachers are so pressed to get through curriculum and prepare for assessments that they do not feel free to 'chase the rabbits.' This is so sad.

A student might have a personal story that relates to the lesson and that story ends up triggering a discussion that lasts the entire class period. The discussion connects the students to the concept in a personal way and in the end, the 'chase' results in more learning than if the rabbit would not have run wild.

A former colleague of mine, Sherri Engels, once said, "If a wasp flies into the room, you teach insects." In this age of pacing guides and curriculum maps, teachable moments are fading away into the cold world of impersonal, mechanical classrooms.

Many teachers don't understand the nature of learning and think that formal learning is the only appropriate and 'proper' way to learn. Albert Einstein said it best. *"It is a miracle that curiosity survives formal education."*

Our educational system is not designed to produce critical thinkers or people who question the status quo. It is not designed for students who love to think creatively and deeply, or have the intellectual capability to challenge authority and question the purpose in educational activity.

Many creative, deep-thinking students do not fit into the current educational mold and rebel against it. Teachers and administrators quickly discipline these students and if the students do not conform, eventually show them to the door.

Our current educational system is designed to produce compliant, shallow-thinking students who do not question, analyze and evaluate it.

Students move from one class to another at the sound of a bell, playing a quick game of musical chairs, until they arrive at a new class before the next bell rings. The school's schedule promotes punctuality over academic engagement.

'Successful' students learn how to start, stop and shift their cognitive foci every hour or so. There is no reason to get too fired up about any one subject, activity or concept, because the next bell extinguishes the flame.

Students sit in uncomfortable, assigned seats, churn out predictable worksheets, take vague notes, memorize massive amounts of information, hand in quizzes and oh, another bell rings. The dog salivates and . . . sorry, I got confused there for a moment.

Day after day it goes on, year after year. Students figure out how to play the game, most of them anyway. Those who do not figure it out simply give up, if they are not forced out first.

How much real thought occurs in the average classroom across this country? Listen to how a former thirteen-year-old student of mine described her school day:

"Here's my day: I get up, get ready for school, get on the bus, get to school, go to my first class, do what I'm supposed to do, fill out worksheets, take notes, listen to the teacher, and a bell rings; I get up, go to the next class, repeat. Then, the school day ends. On a scale of 1 – 10, the amount of any real thinking required at school is a two. I hardly ever have to think. I can do school without it. I have become more of a robot. I have been trained well. As far as questioning why we study the things we study, I quit doing that a long time ago. It doesn't do any good, so I quit wondering about it; asking that question just makes the teachers mad. I just do what I'm told, I hardly ever see any real purpose or meaning in any

of it."

Why is most of our instruction stuck in the lowest levels of critical thinking? Teachers are all aware of Bloom's taxonomy of thought. Many even have flipcharts or posters of this teaching tool displayed in their rooms.[xl] Why is there such a lack of meaningful thinking in most classrooms?

The easy answer is because it requires effort to think deeply; on the part of both the teacher and the students. It is easy to play in the shallow end of the thinking pool. Swimming in the deeper water takes considerably more effort and practice; however, there are diving boards there that will never be found in the shallow end.

The simplest level of teaching and learning is seen in the memorization of factual information. Remembering the states and capitals, planets of the solar system, and the order of operations in math are examples.

As you move from the lowest level of thought upward you progress from a sheer memory to understanding, applying, analyzing, evaluating and finally to creating something. Most teachers are well aware of that order and recognize its value. But how are most classes, assignments and assessments structured?

Sadly, even at the university level (and often MORE at the university level), a student's ability to memorize and regurgitate facts is the most important skill needed for success. How many times have you memorized information, spit it back out on a test and then forgotten it?

We have all done that plenty of times. How many times have your students done that very thing in your class?

That method may have been a productive way to teach in the past when our country was churning out thousands of laborers who were not required to analyze information, collaborate with others, and keep abreast of the fast-changing technological world. That method still works well today for a part of our student population, but times are changing.

Technology is eliminating the need for many of the positions people once held. Google can give you factual information on nearly any subject more quickly than you can read this sentence. Fast food restaurants are moving closer and closer to fully automated organizations. Assembly line production relies more and more on robotic technology.

A quick internet search of 'job skills for today's worker,' landed me at an official White House press release that states, "Employers value workers who can think critically and solve problems. Many highly-paid occupations require workers with good analytic and interactive skills." [xli]

The obvious question arises. If the executive branch of our country's government says that our educational system must produce students who can think critically and work in teams, why do most of our schools still focus on lower levels of critical thought?

If a student can score well on a multiple-choice state assessment, does that necessarily prepare him or her to be a strong worker in our nation's workforce? Maybe it does. Maybe is does not. Are there students who enjoy thinking, have strong analytical minds and could be the next generation of problem solvers and business leaders who don't score as well on multiple choice assessments? Are there students like that who see the pointless nature of some educational exercises?

Let me call these students the 'square peg students.' Throughout the history of education in this country, the holes in the pegboard have been round. Students who fit into them neatly climb right up the ladder. They figure out how to play the school game. They make the honor roll regularly and are compliant more than not. They are masters of the lower level thinking that is at the heart of most educational settings today.

Too many students who do not fit in the system drop out. They give up. We call them lazy, unmotivated, even slackers. Some of them are. But many of them do not deserve any of those labels.

Many people who have gifts of creativity and deep thought feel trapped by formal education's emphasis on robotic regurgitation. A quick internet search of famous people who dropped out of high school will amaze you; Thomas Edison, Ray Charles, Walt Disney, Princess Diana, George Gershwin, and many more.

The list of people who escaped formal education and impacted the world for good is endless. Do you have the next Thomas Edison in your classroom this year? How about the next Aretha Franklin?

In his 1784 essay titled, *"What is Enlightenment,"* German philosopher, Immanuel Kant, challenged the thinkers of Europe to think for themselves.

"Laziness and cowardice are the reasons why such a large part of mankind gladly remain minors all their lives, long after nature has freed them from external guidance. They are the reasons why it is so easy for others to set themselves up as guardians. It is so comfortable to be a minor. If I have a book that thinks for me, a

pastor who acts as my conscience, a physician who prescribes my diet, and so on--
then I have no need to exert myself. I have no need to think, if only I can pay; others
will take care of that disagreeable business for me. Those guardians who have kindly
taken supervision upon themselves see to it that the overwhelming majority of
mankind--among them the entire fair sex--should consider the step to maturity, not
only as hard, but as extremely dangerous. First, these guardians make their
domestic cattle stupid and carefully prevent the docile creatures from taking a single
step without the leading-strings to which they have fastened them. Then they show
them the danger that would threaten them if they should try to walk by themselves.
Now this danger is really not very great; after stumbling a few times they would, at
last, learn to walk. However, examples of such failures intimidate and generally
discourage all further attempts."[xlii]

Many of Kent's words ring true today. People need to find the courage to think for themselves. The quality of their lives on earth is determined by it.

Before I close this chapter on learning, I have to share ten brain-based learning laws that trump traditional education from an educational blog written by Jeff Hurt.[xliii] I am sharing a portion of this article with permission.

1. Brain science trumps traditional education.

Knowing how the brain naturally operates is similar to knowing the laws of driving. Could you drive without knowing the rules of the road? Sure, you could! Yet, you would probably create a lot of traffic problems. And eventually cause a wreck.

The same applies to presenting to others without knowing how the human brain learns. If you do it, you increase the chance that it won't work well. Unfortunately, the learner is the one that deals with the disaster.

2. Emotions trump facts.

For years we've assumed that dumping data, information and stats on audiences is in their best interest. We believe that we should separate feelings from facts and leave emotions at home.

Wrong! Neuroscience has proven that everything the brain learns is filtered through emotions. There are no exceptions. How we use emotion to aide learning determines learning's success.

3. Talking trumps listening.

Here's the law: the person doing the most talking during an education session is the one doing the most learning. So that's actually the speaker.

We need to create more learning opportunities where the speaker talks for about 10 minutes and then the audience talks to each other. We talk in pairs or small groups so we can understand. We talk so we can remember. We talk so we can process.

No, not Q & A time with the presenter. Then only one person is talking and learning. Peer to peer or small group talking trumps one person asking a question any day!

4. White space trumps information dumps.

Many presenters try to cram as much information and data into their presentation as the time permits. We've assumed that content covered means content learned. We've also assumed that if we cover more content, the listener learns more.

Wrong! The amount of learning directly aligns to the amount of thinking and reflection. We need to create more white space (time for the learner to think) and less pushing of content. The more the learner is allowed to reflect, the more they learn.

5. Images trump words.

We remember images. We forget words. Why? 50%-80% of our brain's natural processing power is devoted to processing sight. That's more than all of our other senses. We actually see with our brains, not our eyes. Likewise, when we hear a word, our brain translates it into an image.

6. Writing trumps reading (and listening).

Most audiences have been conditioned to sit and listen and not do anything else.

We write to remember. We remember because we write.

When we write or type, we are processing information. We are thinking about it and thinking increases the likelihood or retention.

7. Movement trumps sitting.

The longer an audience sits, the less they learn.

From the beginning of time, our bodies and brains were made to move. It's in our genes. We think better when we move. For education, this means getting up and moving across the room to a new table. Finding someone you don't know, introducing yourself and then sharing some new thought.

8. Shorter trumps longer.

Neuroscience has proven that our attention span is ten minutes. After that, our attention starts to wane. Chunking content into ten-minute segments and then allowing learners ten minutes to digest is the best way to learn. Does this mean the three-hour session is dead? Absolutely not. It's just designed differently with lots of breaks to allow time for discussion, reflection and application.

9. Different trumps same.

We notice things that have changed. We ignore things that stay the same. Difference, novelty, uniqueness, contrast and the unexpected juice our brains. Boring is the nemesis of learning.

Example: mandating a conference branded PowerPoint template for all speakers creates an image of sameness in our audience's minds from session to session and shuts down learning!

10. Insight trumps knowledge.

Knowing 2+2=4 is one thing. Knowing how to apply that fact is more important.

Our brains learn information by applying new knowledge to past experience. Gaining insight into how to apply a fact or research is more important to our brain than the fact. Our brains crave meaning!

Wow. Which of these brain-based learning facts surprise you and why? Which ones could easily be applied in your next teaching unit?

Go back and highlight anything that you want to share at a future staff meeting. Understanding how the brain works while learning is crucial for all educators who desire to grow and become even more effective.

Other References: Chapter Ten

Knowles, Malcom. "Informal Adult
Education: A Guide For Administrators, Leaders, And Teachers."
University Of Michigan: Association Press, 1950. Web. April 2012.

Hurt, Jeff. "Ten Brain-Based Learning Laws that Trump
Traditional Education." *Velvet Chainsaw*. 2012.
www.jeffhurtblog.com. Web. May 2012.

President's Council of Economic Advisors. "Preparing the
Workers of Today for the Jobs of Tomorrow." *The White House*. 2009.
www.whitehouse.gov. Web. April 2012.

Mastran, Dave. "Music Matters – Bloom's Taxonomy."
Quaver's Marvelous Blog of Music. 2012. www.quavermusicblog.com.
Web. November 2012.

Chapter Eleven: Assessing Learning

"Measurements are not to provide numbers, but insight."
Ingrid Bucher.

As Robert Mager states in his book, *Making Instruction Work*, "If it's worth teaching, it's worth finding out whether the instruction was successful. If it wasn't entirely successful, it's worth finding out how to improve it."[xliv]

An effective teacher takes responsibility for the learning that occurs in his classroom. As he presents new information, he uses a variety of methods to check and see if his students are 'getting it.'

For years, teachers primarily used quizzes and tests to assess learning. In reality, the tests and quizzes were used to give grades, not assess learning, but I will give teachers the benefit of doubt. Teachers of shop classes, physical education, choir/band, art and home economics were the few exceptions.

I made a decent coffee table in high school shop class and the quality of that table showed what skills I learned. It was obvious I needed to improve my jigsaw capabilities. I scored well enough on the President's Physical Fitness Test in grade school to earn a patch, although my lack of upper body strength kept me from the highest award.

I sang in the choir and played in the band and our performances at contests and concerts reflected what we learned in those classes.

Today we call these types of classes, exploratory or elective classes. In most schools, technology, art, music and physical education classes are not considered part of the 'core' curriculum. I have seen core subject teachers look down their noses at teachers of these subjects like they are somehow less of a teacher. That attitude is a cancer on a school staff.

I am proposing just the opposite. When it comes to assessing learning or determining how much students have learned, core teachers could learn a lot from their colleagues in the elective fields.

A written test is an effective method of assessment, but it is certainly not the only method, nor is it always the best method. This chapter is designed to open educators' eyes to the vastness of the world of assessment. I have placed this chapter toward the end of this book because how a teacher assesses is usually closely related to how she teaches.

A teacher who lectures and requires students to take notes will probably give a written test of some format. A teacher who utilizes a variety of teaching strategies in an attempt to reach all her students more effectively will probably have a much larger collection of assessment tools at her disposal.

Before teachers teach any particular unit, topic or skill, they should have a clear picture of the end result of that unit or lesson. Teachers today have curriculum standards and specific teaching outcomes in place from their national, state or local governments.

Most of us know exactly what we are supposed to teach. Will students need to understand Newton's Laws of Motion? Will they have to know the Bill of Rights? Will they have to work three-digit division problems with a decimal? Will they have to know propaganda techniques? That is the easy part.

The much more difficult part is checking to see if students are actually learning what you are teaching. I am not just referring to state assessments that act as summative assessments at the end of a school year. There are other formative assessments of all types, the check-ups that can and should be a constant part of any teaching lesson or unit of study.

Perhaps I should differentiate between the two assessment types. After looking through several definitions, these give the clearest descriptions of the two types of assessments.[xlv]

"Formative assessments are on-going assessments, reviews, and observations in a classroom. Teachers use formative assessment to improve instructional methods and student feedback throughout the teaching and learning process. For example, if a teacher observes that some students do not grasp a concept, she or he can design a review activity or use a different instructional strategy. Likewise, students can monitor their progress with periodic quizzes and performance tasks.

The results of formative assessments are used to modify and validate instruction."

"Summative assessments are typically used to evaluate the effectiveness of instructional programs and services at the end of an academic year or at a pre-determined time. The goal of summative assessments is to make a judgment of student competency after an instructional phase is complete. For example, in Kansas (I changed the state), the state assessment is administered once a year - it is a summative assessment to determine each student's ability at pre-determined points in time. Summative evaluations are used to determine if students have mastered specific competencies and to identify instructional areas that need additional attention."

Keeping with my goal of providing simple, practical tools for educators, I am providing a list that demonstrates the wide variety of assessments, both of the formative and summative type. Locate your trusty highlighter again and mark away.

1   - Hold class discussions or debates

2   - Write essays

3   - Reflect in journal or log entries

4   - Write letters to the editor of a newspaper

5   - Present a proposal to the teaching staff

6   - Prepare a presentation for a school board meeting

7   - Prepare a book review (or article), perhaps a book report for other grade levels

8   - Write a newspaper article for the local or school newspaper

9   - Put a video together explaining a personal position on a difficult topic

10 - Complete a science experiment or other investigations

11 - Create a Power Point or Prezi project

12 - Design a brochure

13 - Develop a Consumer Report type of article evaluating a product

14 - Analyze the school budget and present findings

15 - Film a commercial that 'sells' a learning concept from a time in history

16 - Dress up and act out the life of a person in history

17 - Perform a demonstration in front of the class

18 - Role Play

19 - Produce a poster

20 - Write up a lab report

21 - Prepare an illustrated manual on using the equipment, for a particular audience

22 - Produce a portfolio of work, pictures or data

23 - Take a written exam (the old-fashioned test has its place)

24 - Give an oral examination

25 - Devise an encyclopedia entry

26 - Produce an A - Z of ...

27 - Add short answer questions: True/False/ Multiple Choice

28 - Write a song, rap or poem

This list of examples of assessment tools could go on and on. If you are interested in these thoughts here, please do some research and discover some ways to assess learning that match your curricular area, your teaching style and your students' learning styles.

My challenge to you is to use constant and consistent methods of assessing students. Moments as simple as a question/answer session help you, as the teacher, evaluate the effectiveness of your lessons and units. If your students are not 'getting it,' you need to do something different.

Contrary to the thinking of some teachers, having half of your students fail your class is not the students' fault. If a teacher is responsible for the learning in her classroom, when students do not get it, the teacher has failed.

Just as teachers should present lessons using a variety of strategies, they should also assess their students' learning using a variety of assessing tools.

Other References: Chapter Eleven

Mager, Robert. *Making Instruction Work*. Center for Effective Performance. Second Edition, 1997. Print.

Nightingale, P., Te Wiata, I.T., Toohey, S., Ryan, G., Hughes, C., Magin, D. *"Assessing Learning in Universities."* Sydney, Australia: University of New South Wales Press. 1996. Print.

Chapter Twelve: Leaning on Your Colleagues

"Individual commitment to a group effort - that is what makes a team work, a company work, a society work, a civilization work."
Vince Lombardi

This chapter is another that is so important it could be an entire book in itself. In fact, the more I worked on this chapter the more I realized the need for an entire book devoted to positive teaching teams and their development.

I am afraid that too much in-depth focus on teaching teams within this particular book will muddy the waters and take away from the individual teacher's pursuit of becoming a more effective educator. But because a teacher can become so much more effective through the collaboration of a great team, a brief look into this subject is necessary in these pages.

No teacher who is truly effective can be so by himself. The teaching career revolves around relationships with people. If you are not a people person, you are in the wrong profession. Get out now and do something else; please, for the sake of your students and colleagues.

As I shared in my introduction to this book, much of my effectiveness as an educator has come from the people I have worked with at school. I have been very fortunate to have worked with so many effective and excellent educators. But there is more than good fortune involved.

Realizing the tremendous effect on learning that results from close-knit teams of teachers, I spent the past fifteen years secretly (and sometimes not so secretly) encouraging the teachers I worked with to come together in more personal, professional and productive ways. Perhaps this was the coach coming out in me.

Along with my 34 years in the middle school classroom, I coached several sports at the middle school and high school level. I played college basketball – well, I did not play much, but I was on the team for four years. In those years as an athlete and then later, as a coach, I saw the incredible value of strong teams.

I noticed the benefit of strong school staffs and teaching teams along the way, as well. Students simply learn best when their teachers work together in collaborative and productive ways.

If the teachers you work with are just a group of people who gather at school each day, do their separate jobs and then leave at the final bell, this chapter might be a huge turning point in your school.

Do not tell me about the old, cynical teacher who has no desire to work in a team who is across the hall from you. I know. Do not tell me about the younger, know-it-all teacher who does her own thing and thinks she is better than everyone else. I know about her, too.

This chapter is not going to transform your staff or team overnight and not everyone will be on board; in fact, some will not even come to the station. But it will make a difference for a few teachers, including you. Any major transformation starts with small changes. Let us take a brief look into this subject of colleagues and teaching teams and take the first bite out of the elephant.

A group - in a school setting - is a set of people with individual objectives who happen to share the same boss, the same workplace or are part of the same organizational unit. In a group, individuals might even have the same objectives, but they also might not. At school, teachers might have very similar goals but they may also compete against each other rather than cooperate. If you have taught long enough you know what I mean.

A team is a group that works towards a single, common objective. In fact, the group members might have different individual objectives but those objectives contribute to the higher collective one. In today's educational world, one teacher simply cannot accomplish all of the requirements of the job without help. An effective teaching team shares the accountability for student achievement.

What are a few simple ways to improve the effectiveness of a teaching team?

First, develop relationships that matter. Teachers have to make time to get to know their colleagues. I am not talking about divulging all the intimate parts of life, although a bond just might be produced that provides personal support too.

Professionally, teachers who work together should know each

other's personalities, learning styles, interests and passions. Teachers should know each other's strengths and weaknesses and should be transparent and open enough to admit weakness and seek help from each other.

Relationships grow best in the right soil and they take some time to mature. Someone on the team (probably you) needs to be the one to encourage frequent and gradual sharing sessions. Egos need to be set aside and stories need to be shared. A simple question at lunch (I hope you get to occasionally eat with a few of your colleagues) such as, "What was it like growing up in your home?" is a safe, simple way to help your colleagues open up a bit.

You be the one to pull the lawnmower cords and then sit back and listen to the engines roar. Get your colleagues to talk about themselves and value their words. Admire their stories. Honor their struggles, accomplishments and backgrounds.

Getting people to talk about themselves and getting others to really listen and value each other is half the battle. When people begin to value each other, a fabulous transformation is set in motion. Walls begin to come down and egos begin to fade. You can only imagine what might happen to a teaching team or staff without walls or egos. Think about it for a minute.

Another way you can help build stronger relationships between your colleagues is to ask for help. Your older colleagues have a great deal of experience and wisdom and your younger colleagues have incredible technological skills and fresh ideas. Go to them and ask for help with something. You will be amazed at how quickly that changes the work place atmosphere.

That is not easy. You have to check your pride and allow yourself to be vulnerable. Asking for help and advice in the American culture is seen more as a sign of weakness than a collaborative skill. I say it is a sign of strength.

Effective individual teachers do not necessarily make effective teaching teams. You could have a group of Teacher-of-the-Year award winners who cannot or do not work well together. Athletic teams made up of all-star players do not always win championships. A team made up of average players can be more effective if everyone pulls together.

Why is teamwork so important?

1 - Teamwork improves the school atmosphere.

2 - Teamwork improves communication.

3 - Teamwork helps lower stress.

4 - Teamwork improves productivity.

5 - Teamwork improves insight into student learning

6 - Teamwork improves student achievement.

Quite often the most valuable team members are somewhat disconnected to the core of the team. Due to the location of their work (physical education teacher in the gym) or the school schedule (band teacher has class during core teachers' lunch) certain members of your team often feel alienated. This is usually unintentional, but is still something to be considered.

How often have you heard another colleague make a statement

like, "It's just P.E." or, "Let's schedule the assembly during the band/choir period because music isn't a real class."? Those exact words probably did not come out of their mouths but the attitude behind them probably has. Nothing is more detrimental to the development of a great teaching team than the exclusion of others or the arrogant 'my class is more important than yours' attitude.

Some of my greatest ideas have come from fellow teachers, para-professionals, secretaries, cooks, custodians, or tech experts. A person's value in a school has very little to do with position, title or even educational IQ. A powerful teaching team understands this.

At this moment, please take a couple of minutes and write out the names of any teachers on your staff or team who might feel excluded or disrespected as a result of their position. If you are reading through this book as a staff study, just ask the question. On every school staff, I am fairly sure there are a few people who feel excluded in some way. That should not be. Acknowledge it and fix it.

On most teacher teams, there is usually someone who does not say much. I like to call that person the 'mouse.' That individual just might be the most valuable person in the whole group but because she does not feel accepted or worthy, her contributions are limited.

Sure, it is the responsibility of that person to speak out and to contribute, but it is also the responsibility of the team to encourage that person and include her in the activity of that team. The mouse might hold the key that unlocks your team's magical kingdom.

Teachers on effective teaching teams share a common vision and are committed to reaching that vision. They understand their roles and know when to get help from a colleague who is better at something.

When conflict arises, and it will, an effective team deals with it openly and fairly with a goal of a 'win-win' outcome. Each member of a strong teaching team contributes ideas. There is mutual respect in the team. There is also a lot of laughter.

According to Bruce W. Tuckman, a well-respected psychologist from Princeton University, the process of building a strong group normally involves four stages.[xlvi]

Forming – The group comes together at the start.

Storming – There is natural tension between personalities.

Norming – A common vision or purpose is understood and shared.

Performing – Productivity and effectiveness increase.[xlvii]

I could not agree more with Mr. Tuckman's theory. Most teams get stuck in the storming stage. The team members' individual egos and personalities clash and there is no willingness to change. However, any team that can fight through the storming stage and begin to share common visions accomplishes much more.

One of the quickest ways to improve the quality of your instruction is to begin taking advantage of the experts who teach in your school. Learn to value each other, support each other, depend on each other and challenge each other.

Building a positive and productive teaching team takes some work, a lot of humility and time. But it also takes much of the stress away and adds an amazing human connection to your career. It makes coming to work a lot more fun too.

Other References: Chapter Twelve

"Forming, Storming, Norming, and Performing; Helping New Teams Perform Effectively, Quickly." *Mind Tools Ltd.* www.mindtools.com. Web. June 2012.

"Team versus group, implications for leaders." *Leadership Development Coaching.* 2011. www.leadership-development-coaching.com. Web. June 2012.

Chapter Thirteen: Dispelling Harmful Myths and Dangerous Habits

"Most people don't have that willingness to break bad habits. They have a lot of excuses and they talk like victims."
Carlos Santana

"Don't smile until Christmas."

"Don't get emotionally involved with your students."

"Don't be friends with your students."

"Don't let parents get involved."

"If you give an inch they will take a mile."

"Make an example out of one student."

"Keep them busy."

"Never argue with a student."

"Never show weakness."

"Command respect."

You have heard them all. They are the rules of the teaching road. Veteran teachers are quick to fill the heads of new teachers with these bits of advice. Administrators remind their staffs of them every new school year. Like a good teacher, I tried to follow most of these things for the first fifteen years of my career.

Then I started realizing how ridiculous many of them seemed. In order to evaluate the effectiveness of such guidelines, let us consider a few of these 'rules' and analyze reasons so many support them. Imagine the following words coming from the mouth of a stern, grumpy veteran teacher, at the first meeting of the year.

"Teachers are not friends with students nor should they ever be. A teacher who connects closely with his or her students is unprofessional and somehow destroys the separation between teacher and student. The students then take advantage of the teacher and chaos ensues."

"If teachers get too worried about the details that affect their students' lives they would be so weighed down they would burn out or lose their ability to make objective decisions regarding those students. Discipline issues arise, hampering the learning process."

"If your first few weeks of interactions with your students are like a Marine boot camp then your classroom management problems will be eliminated and your teaching effectiveness will increase."

"If you give the students enough busy work to do, more than they can finish in your class, they won't have time to cause any problems."

"Even when a student has a valid position, never argue with a student. Never admit weakness and always keep the power firmly in your control. If your students sense they have the power they will run the class. Arguing with students makes students think they have some say in their education."

"The more you let parents become involved in their children's education the more problems you will have controlling your class. Parents have no clue about education and must be kept at arm's length or they will think they have some say in the education of their children."

"A quiet and orderly classroom is essential for learning. Movement and talking create discipline issues and the stiller and quieter you keep students the better off your class will run."

How many of those have you heard? My question for you is, 'What is the common denominator in each of the previous statements?' If you answered power, control or discipline, you would be correct. Please, before I go any further into this, I must say that very little learning can take place in a classroom that is wild, chaotic and out of control; I covered that earlier. So, do not get me wrong.

A classroom that is poorly managed will not allow for effective learning. And poor teachers can and do lose control of their classes which results in huge drops of effectiveness. Parents can become too involved and a few helicopter parents can make life miserable. All of those possibilities are granted. But hear me out.

Over the course of my career, I have seen just about every teaching style there is. I have seen teachers who act like drill sergeants and teachers who had no ability to manage a classroom. Neither extreme is good, logical or right. I am going to focus on the drill sergeant mentality here because that is what is often recommended for beginning teachers or teachers who are having some classroom management issues.

As I shared in chapter five, I consider the connections teachers make with students to be the single most important aspect of the teaching/learning process. Show me a teacher who is cold, disconnected and unapproachable and I will show you a teacher who could be much more effective.

Certainly, a rough, tough, 'my way or the highway' teacher

probably has a quiet and orderly classroom but the regimental aspect of his teaching blocks much of the learning. People learn best when they are emotionally connected to the teacher, the material or in the best cases, both.

Teachers often spend more time with young, developing children than their parents do. No one could argue that teachers should be important role models. We are called to model behavior that demonstrates strong character traits. Empathy is an important one.

Without empathy it is very difficult to relate to and connect with other people. Without empathy it is easy to be arrogant and cold-hearted. No one likes to be around a cold, hard, arrogant and selfish person. You would think that one of the worst descriptions for a teacher would be that she was cold, hard, arrogant and selfish.

I am picturing a job interview. Please join me. Administrator: "What qualities do you have that would make you the best candidate for this job?" Candidate: "Well, I'm cold, hard, arrogant and a bit selfish. I try to keep my distance from everyone I am around. I don't smile often and if you don't do exactly what I say, there will be heck to pay." Administrator: "Wow, it looks like you are exactly the kind of teacher we want on our staff."

True, teachers are not - and should not be - 'friends' with students in the sense of a BFF kind of relationship. (BFF = Best Friends Forever) But teachers do not have to be a BFF to care and connect with students.

Teachers should be able to recognize and react with compassion when a student is going through a difficult time. A teacher can still be an authority and provide real concern and support for his or her students.

I spent many years laughing with students, encouraging, supporting, defending and caring for them and not once did I ever feel like I was not the authority or that I lacked the proper objectivity that was required in that position.

My students liked me because I liked them. I had a couple colleagues look down their noses at my relationships with students and thought I was out-of-line. Phooey. It is much more out-of-line to work in such an important position and be cold and unapproachable.

Did I have the quietest class in the building? Nope. Did I have the most obedient students? Again, probably not. What I did have were students who were respectful, engaged and usually interested in learning. I did not get that respect because I commanded it; I got respect because I gave it to my students first. My students knew how much I cared about them and they worked hard because they mostly did not want to disappoint me.

If you are a teacher and you do not like young people or do not really care about them as people, find another job where emotional distance is a requirement.

My final thought in this chapter is on the questionable teaching strategy of 'keeping 'em busy.' Again, let me start by saying that students SHOULD be engaged and involved in classroom activities. Active engagement and involvement DOES help in the management of a classroom. I am all for both of those important truths.

What I am not for is the 'busy' part of the equation. If 'busy' means stimulating, purposeful and practical activity, I am right there. If it means 'busy work' or boring, pointless or impractical work just to keep the class quiet, I most certainly am not.

Again, if producing compliant, quiet and robotic students is the goal, many teachers are on the right track. If we are striving to produce a society in which no one ever challenges or questions the status quo, we are doing an outstanding job. If our aim is to produce people who think for themselves, make future decisions and hopefully change the world for good, I would say we need a revolution.[xlviii]

Other Reference: Chapter Thirteen

"Teacher Myths." *Topical Teaching – Time to Challenge the Stigma of the Classroom.* 2011. www.topicalteaching.com. Web. June 2012.

Chapter Fourteen: Recognizing the Impact of School Culture

"Most businesses repress our natural tendency to have fun and to socialize. The idea seems that in order to succeed, you have to suffer. But I believe you do your best work when you are feeling enthusiastic about things."
George Zimmer, CEO of Men's Wearhouse

I can walk into any school and know immediately if I want to be there or not. Many of you can do the same and so can parents and students. There is a 'feel' in the air - a sense of what the school is about that is on display in the faces of the people and the items on the walls. Are the people smiling and energetic? Do the students seem to enjoy being there? Is there student work on the walls? Do the people work together? Although school climate tends to describe the 'feel' of a school at any given time, school culture defines a larger picture.

Nadine Engels describes school culture as "a shared sense of purpose and values, norms of continuous learning and improvement, collaborative collegial relationships... and sharing experiences."* Other crucial factors that contribute to a positive school culture are effective leadership, a strong understanding of motivation and a sense of belonging. The next four chapters of this book focus on these aspects of a school's climate and culture.

Do you remember the theme song from the old *Cheers* sitcom?

"Sometimes you want to go where everybody knows your name,
and they're always glad you came.
You wanna be where you can see,
our troubles are all the same,
You wanna be where everybody knows your name." *

People want to be around other people who know them, are glad to be around them and who share the same kinds of struggles of life. Show me a school where the people (students, teachers, administrators) are like this and I will show you a great school culture. I would also predict that there is a lot of learning going on there too.

There is a line in Judy Garland's *'Somewhere Over the Rainbow'* song from *The Wizard of Oz* that is equally applicable.

"Somewhere over the rainbow skies are blue,
And the dreams that you dare to dream really do come true." **

All people have dreams. Some have no idea what they are, but all of us share this human trait – we want to accomplish things in life. These dreams might be small – be the first person in my family to graduate from high school – or they might be large – start my own company. Students have these dreams and so do teachers. I'm sure administrators have dreams as do parents and everyone associated with education.

Planted deep inside each of us is a desire to matter – to make a difference somehow. We all would love to be in an environment where those dreams are identified, valued and shaped. Everyone in a school should dare to dream great things and know the people around them will help them reach those dreams.

People matter - every single one of them. Old people matter. Young people matter. Race, gender, age, economic status, or family background should never be a reason for one person to devalue another as somehow less human. We all should matter – every day.

Of all the places where people should be recognized and acknowledged as being valuable as humans, it should be at school. Right? Wrong.

Typical education far too often involves adults who view students as objects and instruments to be used, controlled and filled. In too many schools across our land, a majority of students take on a passive, compliant role - willing to become a hypnotized robot in exchange for movement through the system. Most students learn how to come to class, sit quietly, take notes, complete assignments, go home and repeat again the next day. Those who don't conform are eventually directed to the exit door either temporarily or permanently.

This dehumanization of students is one of the great travesties of our time. Teachers view students as a class of lesser humans who come to school like empty vessels or blank slates, with nothing to offer in the way of knowledge or experience. Although we all know, as humans, that making connections with each other is important, teachers forget. The freedom of students is strictly limited and student autonomy is seldom ever considered.

The direction of information in classrooms nearly always flows from teacher to student. The teacher talks, the student listens. The teacher commands, the student obeys. The teacher questions, the student answers. The freedom of students is limited. Student creativity and self-expression are seldom noticed. Nearly everything in school is set up to establish the teacher > student concept.

There can be a better way. We can all remove the veil that blinds us to others. We can learn to see outside of our own world. We can discover the value of every person, regardless of age, and enjoy the diversity that surrounds us. Teachers and students can become 'we' instead of 'me and you.' Teachers can learn as much from students as students learn from teachers. The trivial transfer of information between disconnected 'machines' can become real moments of real thought between people. Students will be described by their personalities and abilities and not by data points or assessment score categories.

Classrooms could become places where both students and teachers become investigators. Dialogue between the two will never exist in a setting of dominance and submission. Two-way respect grows when teachers quit being hypocritical – saying one thing and then doing another. False love, posters on the wall and fake humility won't create trust and respect.

People will never be finished beings, at least on this earth. We each have different starting points, but we are all on the same road together. People need to see that their futures are changeable; they need to see that they can make decisions that matter. When teachers fail to allow students to make decisions, eventually the students will feel more like objects than humans. No one can be human when preventing others from being so.

I can't think for you or even without you; nor can you think for me or without me. Teachers and students should remember this - every single day. Students can think and they love doing so. Students do have experiences, background knowledge and interests. If allowed, they can be curious, excited, and brilliant. The power of critical thinking is so powerful that some teachers use anything to distract students from doing it. People who think are dangerous.

It doesn't take students long to discover that they aren't supposed to think at school, they are there to comply. After a few years, the students get numb. Like many welfare programs that numb the oppressed, distracting them from the true causes of their problems and from solutions, schools eventually blind students to the problems in the system.

Poor teachers and leaders are out to conquer others, from the toughest to the easiest. These poor leaders certainly don't want or let their subjects to unify and they keep them divided. Cooperation can only happen through communication and vice versa. That can happen and already does in many fabulous classrooms each day. But if teachers don't become owners of their teaching, all reform will be ineffective.

Schools who have a positive climate and culture reap the benefit in many ways. Professional development events produce more positive changes. Community relationships strengthen. Students learn more. Teachers enjoy teaching. Everyone flourishes in the midst of a positive school culture. If your school culture is lacking, you can be sure that many students, teachers and administrators are withering.

The culture of a classroom is the shadow of the teacher. The culture of a school is the shadow of the principal. The shadows that are cast make all the difference in education. Take a step back and examine the culture in your classroom and school carefully. Be honest and take responsibility for shaping a more positive culture in your sphere of influence.

Culture drives expectations and beliefs. Expectations and beliefs drive behaviors. Behaviors drive habits and habits create the future. All consistently successful organizations have great cultures. The next four chapters of this book will help you develop your own positive culture and in turn, begin to affect the culture of your entire building and district. Get ready, this is about to get serious.

Chapter Fourteen - References

*Engels, Nadine; Hotton, Gwendoline; Devos, Geert; Bouckenooghe, Dave; Aelterman, Antonia
Educational Studies, v34 n3 p159-174 Jul 2008

**"Where Everybody Knows Your Name (Cheers Theme) - Gary Portnoy."

*** "Somewhere Over the Rainbow". music by Harold Arlen and lyrics by E.Y. Harburg.

Chapter Fifteen: Promoting a Sense of Belonging

"People are hard to hate closeup. Move in."
Brene' Brown

Although I have never met Brene' Brown personally, I feel like I know her. Her research and thoughts on vulnerability, empathy and belonging have changed the way I teach and even more, the way I live. Several thoughts in this chapter are taken from Brown's latest book, Braving the Wilderness – The Quest for True Belonging. I encourage each of you to find that book and read it as soon as possible.

Another book that has impacted my teaching and will show up in this chapter is Setting the Table – The Transforming Power of Hospitality by Danny Meyer. Although mostly relating to the world of restaurants and fine dining, so much of Meyer's thinking relates to teaching. I owe a great deal to both of these people and must acknowledge I have 'borrowed' a few thoughts to use here.

We live in a world that is shouting, "You are . . . not attractive enough, too old, too dark-skinned, not skinny enough, not rich enough, not smart enough."*

We are taught to develop a thick skin and not listen to what others say about us. You know the old rhyme – *sticks and stones can break my bones but words will never hurt me.* That is absolutely wrong! The opposite is true. Words can hurt much worse that broken bones. Broken bones can heal over time but harsh words can affect us for a lifetime. If you develop a thick skin to keep things OUT, that same skin also keeps important things IN – love, intimacy, vulnerability, etc.*

I've been with a lot of people as they were dying or close to death. Most of them wish they had more time with their family and friends and the regrets people have are always about relationships. I've never heard anyone say, "I wish I could have owned a new Corvette or I wish my 401 K could have gotten to a million dollars."

You can slowly get rid of your thick skin and you can help your students shed theirs as well. Genuine, authentic and passionate people are the key to teaching. People who are warm, friendly, upbeat and have a twinkle in their eyes, draw others in easily and create an atmosphere of true sharing and caring.

If a teacher is on time, ready to go, excited, listens, and makes adjustments along the way, students 'feel' welcomed and that they belong. Belonging happens when people can totally be themselves and still be a contributing part of the class. If they have to 'fit in,' that means they have to change something about themselves to be a part of the class.

Everyone has a story to tell. We think the most interesting stories are those of celebrities. There are biographies, documentaries, 30 for 30 ESPN stories, etc. We find those peoples' stories fascinating. But, do you know YOU have just as fascinating a story to tell . . . probably MORE fascinating than many of the celebrities? If I had an hour with you, I'd know a lot of your story. You wouldn't even know I was learning your story at the time – we would just be talking.

Well, you would be doing most of the talking and I would be really listening and questioning; but, during the hour, you would KNOW you were being valued as a human and you would KNOW that I was genuinely interested in you and your life. And you would leave our meeting feeling valued and encouraged. How do I know that?

Because I've spent the last few years listening to peoples' stories and being absolutely amazed by them. I can find a pearl or two of inspiration or encouragement or wisdom from everyone, although that isn't the reason I listen. I listen simply because I want you to tell your story – the good and the bad – and know someone else is interested.

At the end of the hour, you would feel like you 'belong' with me a little. You would feel like you could be 'real' and that my value of you is not conditional on anything on your end. There is a POWER in being valued, listened to and 'seen.'

Even in the context of poverty, violence, human rights issues, the most hurtful thing is not belonging - especially in a family (have any of you felt the pain of not belonging in your family?) but also in a place of work or as a student in a classroom.*

Remember kickball as a kid at recess? Captains choose sides and the others have their hands up, "Pick me!" Captains pick the people they want to 'belong' or be on their team and at the end there are a few neither captain wants. "You can have them." "I guess I'll take Jimmy," with a sigh. The game starts and Jimmy ends up in right field, kicking last. "Easy out," the other team shouts. "Everybody, move in close." Jimmy proves to be an easy out and there is laughter all around.

Let's say Jimmy goes back into class and the teacher asks for students to read aloud. Jimmy isn't a great reader so he never volunteers. When he is called upon to read, he panics and stutters around, causing everyone to laugh at him again. Let's also say that happens more often than not in Jimmy's world. Assuming everyone has a need to be valued, listened to and 'seen,' what can we expect from Jimmy before too long?

Jimmy will find a way to be 'seen' and valued. Class clown? Sure. Tough kid? Maybe. Smoking in the boys' room? Perhaps. Suspended for cussing out a teacher? Cool. Harm himself and/or others with violent behavior? Tragic.

Many other students like Jimmy will just become invisible, live in a shell, start missing school, being a loner during recess, and sitting by themselves at lunch. They don't belong at the popular table, they don't belong with the athletes or the pretty girls or the band kids or the rednecks . . . they don't 'belong' anywhere. They might try to 'fit in' but they certainly don't belong. Occasionally, a few of them find each other and become a group of 'loners' . . . the 'fringe' group who has its own way of being seen.

How much do students belong in your class? Do your introverted students belong? Do the gifted students belong? The struggling students? The apathetic? Those with learning disabilities?

At the university level, this isn't quite as noticeable due to a number of variables, but the need to 'belong', be valued and seen is still there. The easiest place we can make sure our students belong is in our classroom.

Before any educational expert ever talks about rigor and relevance, she should always talk about how to help your students belong in your class.

Have you ever been to a restaurant and although the food was fine, you didn't 'feel' like you were valued? Your server wasn't cheerful, he didn't apologize for mistakes, the place was too loud or too cold - you almost felt 'invisible.' In that experience, the restaurant provided service (you got your food) but they didn't provide much hospitality.

Have you ever gone to a doctor who had no bedside manner? You didn't feel listened to, in fact, the doctor didn't seem to have time for you. She gave a couple of suggestions, prescribed a medication (service) but you left frustrated. You weren't listened to and you didn't feel like the doctor valued you at all (hospitality).

There is a big difference between service and hospitality. Service is the technical delivery of the 'product.' Hospitality is how the delivery of the 'product' makes its recipient 'feel.' Both are important.**

In education, we can learn from this. Although I agree education is NOT a business, there are certainly aspects to businesses that do apply – and the things that make a successful business are also found in successful teaching.

I must ask, "How do your students FEEL about you and your class?" Service is a monologue – one person talks 'to' the group. Hospitality is a dialogue – the ability to listen to the students and sense things from their perspective. Hospitality can only exist where there is human dialogue and empathy.**

Teachers can cover content (that's what many think it means to teach) but unless they are hospitable, the teaching will always be less than effective. Students need teachers to feel that their teachers are on their sides. Students need to feel that teachers' actions are 'for them,' not 'to them.'

Be proactive with hospitality. Try to genuinely connect with each student at least once a week in some way. Make a comment, give a compliment, question new glasses, listen in on a birthday discussion, etc. It's not hard, but it does require some intentional effort.

I want my class to be anything but average. I want my students to leave class feeling like I designed that day just for them. I want the people to be valued and to think critically. And – on top of that - I want them to spread hospitality to everyone else in the room. Everyone is 'above the line' as I shared earlier in the book.

It is not the teacher's job to impose his needs onto the students - it is the teacher's job to learn to be aware of the students' needs and adjust accordingly. When it comes to hospitality – <u>one size fits one</u>!**

We should imagine that every student comes into our classrooms wearing this invisible sign, *"Make me feel important today."** The teachers who can do that consistently are those who have learned that real effectiveness is rooted in relationships.

Despite all the new technology and cultural changes, teaching will always be a hands-on, high-touch, people-oriented system. Nothing can replace shaking hands, smiling, looking them in the eyes, welcoming them with sincerity, . . . hospitality is not something you can stamp out on an assembly line. If I want my students to take an interest in my class I'd better take some interest in them.

Connections also bring people together. Hobbies, family situations, work, hometowns, age, etc. Help as many as possible find some common ground with others in the room. I use Facebook to gather information about my students before the first day of class.

Me, on the first day of class: "I know a little about you - you like to ride horses." Student: "How did you know that?" Me: "I have magical powers." Listen, remember, use your imagination and connect the dots.

Ten years ago, a sweet, young seventh-grade student told me on the first day of class that she loved cheese snacks. Every Christmas since that day, 'Santa' has showed up at her house delivering a cheese surprise. Ten years have passed and Bailey is now 22 years old. I have connections with hundreds of former students and players and many are cemented by a story or event we shared. You will never be able to connect with your students if you stay on the 'teacher side' of your desk or podium.

The wall between instructors and students is large – teachers have all the power and students have none. Teachers must do what we can to knock down that wall that separates our students from us. We forget that although we have bachelor's degrees, master's degrees and in many cases doctorates, and that our students are in many cases just starting their educational journeys, we share a human connection and spirit. those students come into our rooms, at that point we are ALL part of the same story – we've become a character in theirs and they become the same in ours.

In many classrooms, there is an US vs. THEM mentality, which creates disconnection. Yes, we ARE different in many ways, but under it all we are deeply connected. When we refuse to 'value' a group, it is easy to dehumanize (morally exclude) them.

There is a lot of zero-sum game thinking in education. If the students get any power – the teacher loses. Changing a due date or the guidelines for an assignment - even when those changes are warranted - is unthinkable to many teachers.

More than anything, it seems that the teacher must always be 'large and in charge.' However, the teaching/learning process is not a zero-sum game. When the teacher wins, the students should also. When the students win, so should the teacher.

Connecting with people and building meaningful relationships doesn't just happen. We have to be intentional about it and we have to practice it. Teachers can learn to be present with students without losing who we are or what we want to accomplish. We can learn how to question, listen and be more curious than defensive. We need to try to get students to believe we are in their corners. And we certainly don't want our students to think, 'what is important to me is NOT safe with this person in this setting.'

Get your teacher radar on and start picking up all the clues. Hunt for details – impatient glances at a watch, side discussions, confusion, boredom, frustration, in need of comfort, daydreaming. Each detail provides insight into ways to connect. You will pick up birthdays, hobbies, family members, pets, cars. Listen and store those things away. You don't even have to remember who it was specifically – when something comes up that relates to orchestras (for example), you can just ask, "I remember someone in here plays the violin – who is it? Tell me about this."

It is human nature for us to take as much interest in a teacher if the teacher is taking interest in us. There is no stronger way to build relationships than by taking a genuine interest in other human beings and allowing them to share their stories. When that happens in a classroom, a sense of community and shared ownership happens.

The most effective teachers work FOR and WITH their students. Knowledge and thought flows freely in all directions in those classrooms. Teachers who are not as effective teach TO their students. The flow of knowledge and thought is a one-way street – the teacher is pouring from his pitcher of knowledge to fill the empty heads of his students. Get students to help you. They can fix our technology issues, pass out stuff, share ideas about an activity, lead a discussion, provide a brain break . . . etc. You would love for your students to talk about your class as 'theirs.' Imagine a tweet . . . 'In my speech class today, we learned some really cool stuff.' Students will share things about your class with their friends and the main thing they will share is how they feel important and loved.

A community of people results in trust, acceptance and appreciation. Just a simple, "Where are you from?" can open up connections.** Commonalities are so important.

A teacher's ability to see, hear and sense what's going on during class should also guide the plan and lesson. "Thanks for being here. This is your class and I know we will all learn a lot from each other." You can start a conversation and you will always learn something. You might learn that the student just wants to be left alone.

Remember 'Connect the Dots' pictures? Danny Meyer, in his book, Setting the Table, talks about connecting the dots with the people in his world. Dots are information bits. The more you collect, the more frequently you can make meaningful connections and get a clearer view of a person; but, you have to collect dots before you can connect them. Teachers should excel in the dot collection process. We should store the dots away and when the time is right, use them to connect with our students. There is an aspect of creativity here, too.

Be curious about your students and colleagues! Learn about their dots. Their information is all in there – you just have to look for it. Be curious about their opinions and positions.

One of the reasons we aren't curious or don't ask questions is because those traits are seen as weakness today. Too many times, if I don't agree with you or something you say, I'm going to quit listening. We should respect each other, question and learn. We can still disagree with someone, but we should at least hear him out and try to understand his position. I wonder how many times a student has a problem or an issue and we refuse to listen because we are too selfish, stubborn or even rude?

Moths are attracted to the light and warmth of a light bulb at night. Both are needed by the moth. In our teaching world, light is 'service' (teaching strategies, lecture ability, technology, etc.) and warmth are human connections and the 'feel' created. Students need both.**

Students come to class to learn, but they also come to be nurtured, although they don't know that. Even though they don't always know they need nurtured, students feel it when it happens and they appreciate it. Have an infectious kind of empathy. No one can be happy and warm all the time, . . . but the key is that when you are in a bad mood or grumpy, that you don't let it ruin the class period. A skunk sprays its enemy but the smell can spread for a mile or two, affecting anyone in the area. A skunk's scent is toxic. Don't be a skunk.**

Leadership is not just measured in what is accomplished, but more in what your people 'feel' while accomplishing things. I've learned to watch things closely – are the students getting to know each other? Are they having fun, thinking and honoring everyone? Are we learning things? Am I boring them to death?

A basketball coach is extremely focused during the first couple minutes of each game. "Don't talk to me, I need to watch, listen, and think." Coaches are carefully watching defenses, offenses, presses, star players, play calls, mismatches, advantages, disadvantages, looks in faces (fear, confidence, comfort, panic), body language – frustrated, down, energetic, or too excited.) THEN – although we have a game plan, there will be a few tweaks (sometimes major tweaks) early. Many coaches call an early time-out as soon as they gathered enough information to recalibrate the plan.

Some coaches are really stubborn – they won't change anything. So are some teachers. "I'm not changing anything, it's up to them to get it." The best coaches make adjustments based on observations.

Many of you probably use a GPS in their vehicles today. You set the trip into the computer and start. If you miss a turn or something unexpected comes up, the GPS has to 'recalibrate.' There should be a lot of recalibrating during each lesson or semester as you gather more information from the students.

Too many teachers set the GPS and disregard the recalibration advice and end up in Salt Lake City when they wanted to go to Cleveland. Or, almost more tragically, they realize with about three class sessions remaining that something hasn't worked. They blame the students and too many fail the course. Gather 'dots,' watch and listen, make connections and make adjustments.

First impressions really do matter. Research shows that a student forms an opinion about a teacher and class within the first few seconds of the first class session. Win the first round if you can. If you can connect with them early, you have a much better chance of keeping them enrolled and then keeping them engaged later.

Do this one thing – do ANYTHING other than read the roster and take attendance at the beginning of the first class. Tell a story, read a book, show a video clip, have the class do an activity, or simply tell why you love this class or subject . . . just don't read through the roster first. You can wait ten minutes to do that. Plus, any late stragglers will have arrived by then. Throw a hook with some bait out into the water and see if you can hook them immediately.

We'd like our students to be proud to identify with us and our classes. If we see their parents or friends, we'd like them to be excited to introduce us. The more we can get the students' connected in the class, the more they will see our class as a part of their own story. When they get asked (and they do) how school is going, you want them to talk about your class with some excitement - even if it is a very difficult and rigorous class. We want to give our students a story worth telling.

A few final and fun suggestions from the book, "Teaching as a Subversive Activity" by Neil Postman:***

1. Don't use textbooks for five years.

2. Have English teachers teach math, math teachers English, social studies teachers - science, science teachers - art, and so on. One of the biggest obstacles is the desire for them to try to get something they think they know into the heads of people who don't know it.

3. Transfer all elementary teachers to the high school and vice versa.

4. Require every teacher who thinks he knows his subject to write a book on it.

5. Dissolve all subjects, course, and course requirements.

6. Limit teachers to three declarative sentences per class.

7. Prohibit teachers from asking questions they already know the answers to.

8. Declare a moratorium on tests and grades.

9. Require teachers to undergo some form of psychotherapy as a part of their in-service training. This would help them come to terms with why they became teachers.

10. Classify teachers according to their ability and make the list public.

11. Require teachers to take a test prepared by students on what the students know.

12. Make every class an elective and withhold a teacher's pay if students don't show interest in going to a teacher's class.

13. Require every teacher to take a leave of absence every fourth year to work in another field.

14. Require teachers to provide some sort of evidence that they have loving relationships with at least one other human being.

15. Require all graffiti accumulated from the school's bathrooms be reproduced on paper and hung in the school's halls.

16. Prohibit the following words and phrases from the school: *teach, syllabus, covering ground, IQ, makeup, test, disadvantaged, gifted, accelerated, enhancement, course, grade, score, human nature, dumb, college material,* and *administrative necessity.* In our era, we might add IEP, 504, alternative assessment, adaptive curriculum, RIT score, college and career ready, tech prep, etc.

17. Teachers should ask, "Why in the world should anybody be 'taught' my subject?"

Chapter 14 - Notes

* Brown, Brene'. Braving the Wilderness: the Quest for True Belonging and the Courage to Stand Alone. Random House, 2017.

**Meyer, Danny. Setting the Table: the Transforming Power of Hospitality in Business. Harper, 2008.

***Postman, Neil, and Charles Weingartner. Teaching as a Subversive Activity. Penguin Books, 1972.

Chapter Sixteen: Unpacking Motivation

"You don't have to see what someone is doing to know if it is his true vocation. You have only to watch his eyes; a cook mixing his sauce, a surgeon making a primary incision, a teacher in front of a class... they wear the same rapt expression, forgetting themselves in a function. How beautiful it is, that eye-on-the-object look."

W. H. Auden

There is a science of motivation and a raft of research available on the topic of motivation but most people ignore it. Most things in our current society are built around extrinsic motivators. The 'If/then world' – IF you do something or don't do something THEN I will reward you in some way – is still the norm. Merit pay, salary hike, bonus pay, grades, scholarships, etc. are all important, but they don't motivate people for the long run and often unintentionally do more harm than good.

If/then motivational strategies do work well for simple sets of rules and procedures, activities that require little or no thought – i.e. repetitive, mundane tasks. Carrots and sticks work well when there is a clear destination involved. Rewards by nature narrow our focus and focus our concentration, but they restrict our possibilities when critical thought is required.

MTSS tiers, GPAs, reading levels, AR reading goals, assessment categories - the brightest students enjoy figuring out how to beat the system and they do so quite well. The struggling students develop a fixed mindset and see themselves as 'less than good.'

This old system of extrinsic motivators worked well for much of the 1900's and still does in some places today. Stickers, candy, and plaques work well for those jobs that require little creativity or thought. Those carrots are also helpful when work doesn't allow for individual discretion or autonomy, and assignments are mostly 'mindless.' But, the world has changed. We live in a new age.

Many of today's jobs require real critical thought and creative, problem-solving capacities. We have the robots to do the dirty work, we have Google to answer our factual information - what we need now are people who can THINK!

Over the years, I have been involved in training sessions and faculty development events where business leaders speak to their needs in employees. Although nearly all say that good grades *might* help an applicant get a foot in the door, it isn't grades that 'win' the job.

Employers today are looking for self-motivated, critical thinking, creative problem-solvers who are able to work both independently and in groups. Most aren't looking for assembly-line workers who are motivated by sweeter carrots.

Back in the day, school was like this. Students were treated like assembly-line workers. We filed in quickly and quietly before a bell, took our seats, completed our mostly mindless work, turned it in and then left. We didn't question the purpose for the assignment, didn't challenge the teacher's thinking, didn't design a new way to complete the work, and we seldom did any real critical thinking.

Compliance and conformity were rules of the day. If we are honest, they still often are. We give stars and candy and extra credit and tickets so students are instantly rewarded. Now, if your class is boring, trivial and mindless – keep doing that. It will work for you. But you better start buying more candy and bigger stickers because extrinsic motivators are addictive and require more and more 'wow' factor to work.

Conversely, if your classroom is exciting, engaging, thought-provoking, creative, problem-solving, etc., stickers aren't needed. Students enjoy being in your room because they are engaged, get to think and see a purpose for accomplishing the work.

The routine, rule-based, left brain work is disappearing at the same rate technology advances. The right-brained, synthesizing and creative kind of work is exploding. The rules aren't as clear. There are hundreds of variables involved in many jobs today; things just aren't cut and dried as they once were. Variability is usually more important than universality. There are laws, medicines and truths that are universal – but even in those situations, a personal application is helpful and/or adds to the effectiveness.

Horizontal segmentation describes the availability of options in peoples' decisions. There used to be just a couple types of spaghetti sauce – meat and no meat. Now you can purchase over fifty different types. Cancer treatment has improved tremendously, mainly because the treatment has become more personal. Consider the different types of coffee, sodas and chips you can buy.

Giving people a range of options (eight options seem to produce the most motivation) and some 'say' in their choices is motivating. That's why pacing guides and scripted teacher texts are often inappropriate because they are a universal application to a diverse and varying event.

We can't give endless options (people don't know what to choose and are less satisfied when they do choose because they know they could have had other options) but we can give a few that most will prefer. Again, the spaghetti sauce story applies as the marketers ended up limiting sauce options to a few, not hundreds.

In a school-related study, scientists examined three groups of students who played different types of games. One group was to be rewarded with a small bonus, one with a medium bonus and one with a large bonus. If a participant scored really high, she got a large bonus.

Here is what happened. If the game involved simple mechanical thinking – like multiplication flash cards – the bonuses worked like we would think. However, the more real thought that was required (creativity, problem solving, etc.) the less the bonuses helped at all. In fact, performance was POORER when higher incentives were given.

In several other surprising research studies, financial incentives have been found to lead to poorer performance. Too many organizations make decisions about their people and performance based on outdated science. As a result, the culture of a place can become toxic. People today are not motivated with sweeter carrots or bigger sticks. Extrinsic incentives often lead to poorer performance whenever critical thought is required.

The current system of rewards and punishment dulls critical thinking and blocks creativity. Incentives and extrinsic motivators - if you do this, you get this - don't last over time. The new and better approach focuses on intrinsic motivation.

The younger generation of workers changes jobs frequently, roughly once every three years. That change is not due to unhappiness or frustration. Many of today's workers simply enjoy accomplishing challenging and meaningful activities. When a job becomes boring and/or meaningless, employees are quick to move onto something different. Today's younger employees want to work because the work matters, because work interests them and because they like the challenge of accomplishing things. The days of the 50-year career, golden watch retirement celebrations are vanishing.

Money DOES matter. We all need it to live. The more we make of it the better, or so it seems. Actually, it isn't quite that simple. If an employer pays workers reasonable salaries – what they deserve or maybe a bit more – that gets a focus on money off the table. Then, it is possible to begin to help them 'see' the importance and purpose of the work.

One Princeton University study* in 2010 found that $74,000 is the optimal amount of annual income for a family of four today. More than that adds stressors related to taxes, investments, etc. and less than that can lead to a lack of certain necessities. According to this study, once a family earned $74,000, their level of happiness remained about the same as those who made millions and in some cases was greater than the wealthy families.

Merit pay for teachers doesn't work. Period. Research shows that merit pay has no impact on learning whatsoever. In some cases, the learning decreased. What we need to do is raise the base pay and get rid of poor teachers. It's not money that makes us happy – it is whether our work fulfills us.

In an increasing number of companies today, workers are given some time to work on anything they want – they just can't work on what they normally do. It might be an entire work day or an hour, but this is something worth considering in schools. Why couldn't occasional in-service days become 'Fed-Ex Days,' where everyone thinks creatively about an educational issue with no restrictions or requirements, except to deliver a new idea the next day. 'Post It Notes' came from IBM's 15 % time-off to brainstorm structure.

Somebody invented management – it isn't a natural thing. One day, management may disappear. Employers are giving more and more autonomy to employees today. Autonomy is valued over time, technique, task, and team. . . it doesn't matter how, when, where or with whom you work as long as you get your work done!

My daughter, Tara, is a CPA and auditor for governmental agencies. She has a great deal of flexibility in her schedule. She can occasionally work from home or take off early as long as she gets her work done.

Microsoft Encarta Encyclopedia paid its employees great salaries. Wikipedia asked for volunteers, people who wanted to work for the fun of it. Which worked out the best?

Here is the old way: Reward an activity and you get more if it – punish an activity and you get less of it. Give kids stickers for each math workbook page completed and for a short time they might work harder, but it won't be long before they lose interest in math. When artists are paid to do a commissioned work, their creativity is often clouded and the process is less enjoyable.

In a story told in the article, The Why Axis: Hidden Motives and the Undiscovered Economics of Everyday Life, a group of day-care centers had problems with a few parents not picking up their children on time at the end of the day. An announcement was sent to parents explaining that the centers were going to start charging parents for each minute they were late. The day-care centers thought it would stop parents from being late. It did the OPPOSITE! Before the new 'fine,' most parents showed up on time because they didn't want to be a burden on the coaches and teachers. Parents had an intrinsic reason to be on time. They cared about the school workers and their time. But, by fining the parents for being late, they took away the intrinsic reason for being on time and shifted it to a financial "I can buy extra time" event.

It pushed the moral obligation out the window and even more parents ended up being late.

For those of you who are parents, you can start with your own children. Give your own children an allowance and some chores but don't combine the two. By linking money to the completion of chores, parents turn allowance into an 'if-then' reward. This sends a clear message – if she doesn't get paid, no kid would willingly set the table, empty the garbage, or make her bed. It converts moral and family obligations into just another financial transaction and teaches that the only reason to do a 'crummy' task for your family is in exchange for money. We need young people to learn the difference between principles and payoffs.

Praise effort and strategy, not intelligence. When children are praised for 'being smart,' they believe each task is a test of whether they are smart or not. So, they resist new challenges and choose the easiest path because they don't want to look dumb. By contrast, children who understand that effort and hard work lead to mastery and growth are more willing to take on new, difficult tasks. There is a lot of fabulous, new research on growth and fixed mindsets. We would like if all our students had a growth mindset and be willing to try, fail, learn and grow. The same holds true for principals and their teachers.

_____

Chapter Sixteen – Other References

The Golden Circle – Simon Sinek (video)

*Do We Need $75,000 to Make Us Happy? – Belinda Luscombe

The Puzzle of Motivation – Dan Pink (video)

How to Be a Leader – Simon Sinek (video)

Flex - Jane Hyun and Audrey S. Lee (book)

Chapter Seventeen: Exploring Teacher Immediacy

"Motivation is getting people to do what you want them to do because they want to do it."
Dwight D. Eisenhower

This chapter is a follow-up to the previous chapter on motivation and could be labeled Chapter 16B. The research is from my master's thesis and has been career-changing for many educators, including myself. Consider this carefully and be honest and vulnerable in regard to your teaching as you read.

Motivation is the desire to do things. Motivation gets people up each morning and guides their directions in life. Although not outwardly observable or easily measurable, motivation is a powerful force that drives achievement. Inspiration, enthusiasm, ambition and determination are all linked to the concept of motivation (Cherry, 2014).

In classrooms all around the world, many healthy, economically stable students from strong families sit unmotivated. Although the exact reasons or causes are often unclear, there are a few that are identifiable.

Unmotivated students might not feel they can do the assigned work or they feel that the work required to complete or even start the task is too great. Students can be unmotivated because classroom instruction is not engaging. A lack of real purpose or payoff turns off many students. Some lack self-confidence and cannot muster the courage to attempt the activity. For others, the lack of a positive teacher/student relationship results in a lack of motivation and interest (Lamm, 2011).

This positive teacher/student relationship – or the lack thereof – is at the heart of this action research project. Theodore Roosevelt's quote, "People won't care what you know until they know that you care," is thrown around schools and classrooms like a banner. Many teachers would claim the Roosevelt quote as their own, but their walk doesn't always reflect their talk. Many teachers take the time to establish and maintain positive connections and relationships with their students while many others seem to have no desire to do so. Many teachers greet their students each day with a smile, hug, story or question. Others teach an entire semester without ever learning to identify their students by name. Some classrooms are warm and inviting while others are cold and sterile.

Does any of this actually have an effect on the teaching/learning process? Do students learn more from teachers who connect with them in positive ways? Are students more motivated to engage in learning activities with teachers who have affirming relationships with them? And put more simply still, do students learn more when they know their teacher cares about them as a person? If the answer to those questions is yes, what specific kinds of teacher behaviors demonstrate a caring connection?

The goal of this study was to consider these questions regarding verbal and non-verbal behaviors between teachers and students and their possible effects on student motivation. Using both quantitative and qualitative observations to analyze the correlation between teacher/student relationships and student motivation this research hopes to shed more light on this important issue and provide practical insight to improve the effectiveness of educators everywhere.

Introduction

Unmotivated students have little or no desire to learn. They are neither enthusiastic nor interested in the task at hand. Students lacking motivation are easily identifiable and even teachers with little or no experience quickly learn to notice the traits (Keith, 1995):

- Listless or lazy behavior
- Apathy regarding work, appearance, and discipline
- Frequent off-task behavior
- Little or no participation in activities
- Late and missing work
- Frequent absences
- Little or no joy expressed in the classroom

There are many possible reasons why a student might be unmotivated. Health issues, difficult family dynamics and socio-economic challenges can result in childhood depression and/or the accompanying lack of motivation it includes (Lovett, 2014). Although critical, the classroom teacher has very little control over those difficult life issues.

What the teacher DOES have control over are the many aspects of and strategies used in the teaching/learning process in his/her classroom that have an effect on student motivation. For this study, teachers' verbal and non-verbal immediacy behaviors were measured and considered in the context of student motivation.

Literature Review - Teacher Immediacy and Student Motivation

"Teacher immediacy is a perception of physical or psychological closeness." (Richmond, 2002, p. 65). Originally, the concept of immediacy focused on nonverbal behaviors; however, today immediacy includes verbal communication as well. A teacher who effectively uses immediacy behaviors shrinks the divide between himself and his students. This review found three identified benefits of immediacy behaviors by teachers:

- Classroom management issues decrease significantly. Teachers who developed high-quality relationships with their students had 31 percent fewer discipline issues that teachers who did not (Marzano, 2003). As opposed to coercive strategies, positive connections with students allow teachers to manage their classrooms more effectively.

- If students see a teacher as uncaring, disconnected or unresponsive, there will be a lack of trust among them in regard to the teacher. Students are drawn toward teachers they trust (Richmond, 2002).

- Teacher immediacy results in a more emotionally 'safe' learning environment and increases the likelihood that greater learning will occur (Witt, P.L., Wheeless, L.R., & Allen, M. 2004).

In a study of immediacy and motivation, Weiner (1992) described what most humans already understand – that human nature tends to seek out activities that are enjoyable, satisfying, and safe, while avoiding those that give pain, discomfort or are threatening in some way. Martin, Myers, and Mottet (1999) discovered that students tend to avoid interacting with instructors who seem uninterested or uncaring, particularly after the students have made repeated attempts to reach out to the instructors.

Identifying immediacy behaviors is challenging. Measuring those behaviors is even a greater challenge. In the same way, identifying and measuring student motivation is equally challenging. But, if this issue of teacher immediacy and student motivation is as important and crucial as it seems, difficulty with quantitative data should not be a deterrent. Fortunately, recent studies have provided several helpful ideas.

Immediacy researchers have attempted to develop a set of scales which can directly identify specific traits such as smiling, vocal expressiveness, and relaxed body position (Gorham, 1988). Once identified, these traits may be observed, recorded, analyzed and improved. Beginning teachers could be taught these valuable behaviors with more specificity. Teachers who struggle with classroom management or student progress could benefit from professional development that focused on immediacy behaviors (Christophel, 1990).

Nonverbal immediacy (or lack of immediacy) behaviors occur without much thought – they 'show' a person's internal feelings and attitudes. In a teacher's classroom, nonverbal immediacy behaviors include actions such as eye contact, body position, physical proximity, personal touch and body movement (Richmond). In an older, but still informative study (Anderson, 1978) a researcher concluded, "The more immediate a person is, the more likely he/she is to communicate at a close distance, smile, engage in eye contact, use direct body orientation, use overall body movement and gestures, touch others, relax, and be vocally expressive." Nonverbal immediacy has been shown to increase all aspects of learning, including students' views of teacher effectiveness (Butland and Beebe, 1992).

Verbal teacher immediacy refers specifically to words used by a teacher, along with the expressions that accompany those words, to develop a positive connection with her students. Expressions that describe or define ownership (I/we compared to my/our) and probability (will/may) have been discovered to provoke positive and negative responses in students (Rubin, 1994).

Verbal immediacy has also shown to be directly correlated to student motivation and increased student willingness to participate in and contribute to class (Christensen, Curley, Marquez, and Menzel 1995). Examples of verbal immediacy include specific praise for student efforts, humor, openness, willingness to engage with students in conversation, and overall joy in meeting with and interacting with students.

Teachers communicate to students all the time, both verbally and nonverbally. Body language, glances, gestures, and facial expressions are just a few common behaviors. These immediacy behaviors, though usually overlooked by the teacher, appear to spread either a positive or negative message to her students. High expectations of academic success and positive behavior is built and developed through consistent, positive and encouraging verbal and nonverbal behaviors. The following immediacy behaviors demonstrated a moderate or higher correlation to teacher immediacy behavior. These behaviors (and the corresponding correlation data) will guide the development of the student survey used in this current study (Velez and Cano, 2008).

- Teacher calls student by first name on a consistent basis.
- Teacher frequently asks students questions that encourage their opinions and thoughts.
- Teacher frequently asks students for input relating to assignments, due dates, topics, etc.
- Teacher gives specific and meaningful praise to students and gives frequent feedback on assignments and work.
- Teacher changes voice, face and body expressions frequently.
- Teacher refers to the class as 'our' class and uses the term 'we.' (Compared to 'my' class and 'I').
- Teacher is available and enjoys talking with students outside of class.
- Teacher uses humor appropriately and there is occasional laughter in class.
- Teacher smiles at students during class.
- Teacher handles class calmly and with patience and body language shows it.
- Teacher occasionally uses appropriate handshakes, high fives or other touches.
- Teacher enjoys being around young people.
- Teacher is more positive than negative.

Millions of dollars have been spent on the development of new standards and assessments. Common Core (College and Career Readiness) standards are the topics of professional development sessions, all with the dream of increasing learning and achievement in public schools. But in spite of all the money, time, effort and stress focusing on math and language curricula, little or no attention is given to the psychological walls that separate many students from deeper learning.

There has been significant research completed that has proven a moderate or greater correlation between teacher immediacy and student motivation. This study adds to that expanding research pool. The importance of this study is obvious. Unless students are motivated to learn and are connected to positive educators who do not just 'talk the talk' of caring, gaps in learning will occur and more and more students will be left behind. Teachers who lack immediacy behaviors create a classroom climate that is uncomfortable for many students - academically, socially and emotionally.

Research Question

To what extent (if any) does teacher immediacy affect the learning motivation of middle school students?

Methodology for Planned Intervention

After being granted permission to conduct the present study with seventh grade students at Circle Middle School by Mrs. Brenda Young, principal, and Mr. Nathan Sherwood, assistant principal, the decision was made to utilize Mr. Bruce Demaree's seventh grade geography students and classes for the research. Mr. Demaree underwent colon cancer surgery (my great friend Bruce passed away a few months after the first edition of this book was printed) and was gone from school for a few weeks, during which time the researcher served as a long-term substitute teacher in his class.

Although the researcher was not a full-time teacher on staff at Circle Middle School, he was very familiar with and comfortable with the students there. As a long-time member of the Circle community and a current coach and substitute teacher, the researcher was considered by most students as a 'regular' teacher in most ways. That familiarity between the researcher and students provided for honest reflections and qualitative observations. The position as a substitute teacher gave the researcher an 'outside' vantage point throughout the study and helped allow for more reliable data collection.

On two consecutive days (A day and B day), all seventh-grade students participated in a 25-question survey during their respective seventh grade geography periods. The survey was designed to evaluate the students' perception of one of their teacher's (2A class) immediacy along with their interest and motivation in that teacher's class. The 2A class was chosen because the second block period included all students in regular classroom settings and eliminated any negative attitudes associated with first period classes. Also, afternoon classes were eliminated as possible test subject periods due to the number of students who left school for extra-curricular activities.

The study was completed in absolute anonymity – students did not write their names on student surveys and no teacher names or subjects were included in any of the questioning. In order to eliminate any bias regarding the researcher's relationships with teaching colleagues, the student surveys were shuffled together at the end of the second day, eliminating any possible identifiable clue. When the surveys were tabulated, the results were valid and reliable.

A brief description of this study was given to each group of students before the survey was distributed. Each of the 25 statements was read aloud by the researcher before the students began completing the survey (see Table 1). If students had any questions, they were answered carefully before the process began. After a reminder regarding anonymity, the students were instructed to complete the survey carefully.

The researcher monitored student effort. If a student appeared to put little or no effort into the survey, that survey was excluded from the study.

Finally, as the third part of the data triangulation process, the researcher used a daily MTSS group of students to gather perspectives, opinions and interview answers. This focus group provided insight from the students' perceptions. The researcher led the discussions that focused on learning, motivation to learn and teacher behaviors related to immediacy. Relevant and insightful quotes from students were recorded for later analysis.

Data Collection Plan

After a brief description of the project/study, students were given the following survey with instructions to complete it as honestly as possible based on their 2A class and teacher. When the survey was completed, it was turned into the researcher and was not viewed at this point, being placed in a file folder until all surveys were completed.

Table 1: - Circle Middle School Student Survey

Please think about your 2A class (or 2nd period communications or math class). Mark the answer that best represents how you feel about each of the statements below using the following opinions.

1 = Strongly Disagree (No way!)

2 = Disagree (Not so much)

3 = Neutral (Not really yes or no)

4 = Agree (Yes, I'd say mostly true)

5 = Strongly Agree (Absolutely!)

----

1. Doing well in my 2A class is important to me. _____
2. The teacher in my 2A class calls me by my first name (either in the hallways or in the classroom) at least once each day or two. _____
3. When I am in 2A I give good effort and try hard. _____
4. My 2A teacher frequently asks the students questions and encourages students to share their opinions or discuss the lesson. _____
5. I am more interested in my 2A class compared to others. I like this class very much. _____
6. My 2A teacher asks the students about their opinions regarding assignments, due dates, discussion topics, etc. _____
7. I care a lot about the grade I get in my 2A class. _____

8. My 2A teacher usually (most days) praises or compliments students' work, thoughts, actions or comments. _____

9. What I learn in my 2A class is important to me. _____

10. The teacher in my 2A class looks at us (as a class and as individuals) when he/she talks. _____

11. My 2A teacher gives me feedback on my work or my thoughts. He or she tells me how I am doing, what I do well and what I need to work on. _____

12. Compared to other classes I try harder in 2A. _____

13. My 2A teacher changes his or her facial expression or changes how his or her voice sounds during class. _____

14. The teacher in my 2A class usually refers to this class as 'our' class or what 'we' are doing, not as 'my' class or what 'I' am doing. The focus in my 2A class on the students, not on the teacher. _____

15. When I am in 2A, I work hard most days. _____

16. My 2A teacher usually seems available and interested in talking to students outside of class. _____

17. My 2A teacher moves around the room quite a bit during class. _____

18. My 2A teacher uses humor in the class and there is frequent laughter in 2A. _____

19. I give my best effort on assignments and activities in my 2A class. _____

20. My 2A teacher smiles at lot during class. _____

21. My 2A teacher handles class issues with patience and calmness. He or she always seems to have things under control. _____

22. My 2A teacher is more positive (complimentary) than negative (critical). _____

23. I get my homework done every day for my 2A class. _____

24. My 2A teacher occasionally (some days) shares appropriate touches with students – high fives, handshakes, pats on the back, etc. in and out of the classroom. _____

25. It is obvious the teacher in this class enjoys young people and enjoys being around them. _____

Statements 1, 3, 5, 7, 9, 12, 15, 19, 23 relate to student motivation and engagement. Statements 2, 4, 6, 8, 10, 11, 13, 14, 16, 17, 18, 20, 21, 22, 24, and 25 relate to teacher immediacy.

Data Analysis Plan

Data from the student survey was gathered, recorded and statistically analyzed. A regression statistical analysis was then used to determine the strength of the correlation between teacher immediacy and student motivation.

My hypothesis was – "If teachers use consistent immediacy behaviors, then their students will demonstrate a greater motivation to learn in their classrooms." This study did not measure cognitive learning - its focus was strictly on motivation and in a related sense, on student engagement during class periods.

Data Analysis

One hundred thirty-five seventh grade students at Circle Middle

School completed the student survey (Table 1) describing their perceptions of teacher immediacy behaviors. The students completed the surveys seriously and considered the statements carefully throughout the fifteen-minute time designated. Two students did not complete the survey – the back side was not finished – and those two surveys were removed from the study.

The anonymity of the entire study was guarded carefully. Students did not write their names on the surveys and they also did not include the name of the teachers they assessed. Due to the researcher's position as a long-term substitute teacher in the seventh-grade geography class - the regular teacher, Mr. Demaree, was out due to surgery - the geography class designated in the study (2A) completed the survey based on their 2B class instead. Therefore, there was no way the researcher knew the identity of either students or teachers, eliminating any possible, unintentional bias rooted in personal friendships.

Two of the student motivation survey statements were removed from consideration after students commented on the unrelated aspect of them.

Survey statements #7 and #23 - *I care a lot about the grade I get in my 2A class,* and *I get my homework done every day for my 2A class,* caused much uncertainty among students. Students commented that they 'care' about their grades in ALL classes regardless of their perceptions of the content or teacher. Students also shared how some classes never had homework (physical education, art, choir, etc.) and that they were confused as to how to respond to that particular statement. After considering the students' concerns and the intention of this study, those two statements were removed before data was analyzed.

Upon completion of the surveys, data was compiled in a spreadsheet. Averages were calculated and the data from both the independent variable (teacher immediacy) and dependent variable (student motivation) was analyzed. The current study considered the possible correlation between teacher immediacy behaviors and their students' motivation to learn. In order to determine whether or not a correlation existed, and if so, how strong the correlation was, Excel data analysis options were used.

First, each data point was transferred into a scatter plot graph, with the teacher immediacy values on the x axis and the student motivation values on the y axis. Immediately, a positive correlation was evident based on the slope angle. With the exception of three outlier points, the remaining 134 points fell along a positive linear slope. The strong and apparent linearity provided a basis to use a regression analysis to determine correlation. (See Table 3)

Table 3 – Scatter Plot Graph

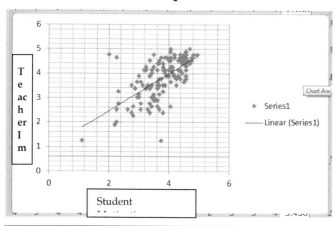

When a regression analysis was used, a striking correlation of .77915 between the two variables of this study was calculated. Using Dancey and Reidy's Correlation Coefficient Categorization (2004), a correlation coefficient of .78 is described as 'Strong.' (Table 4)

Using other tables and categories, a .78 coefficient is consistently described as being 'High' or 'Strong.'

Table 4 – Dancey and Reidy's Correlation Coefficient Categorization Scale

Value of the Correlation Coefficient	Strength of Correlation
1	Perfect
0.7 - 0.9	Strong
0.4 - 0.6	Moderate
0.1 - 0.3	Weak

The R-squared coefficient of .607 between teacher immediacy and student motivation is also significant. Although correlation coefficients involving human behaviors are naturally lower than more quantitative studies, the .61 R-squared coefficient describes a significantly close range between data points across the linear slope.

Although the researcher's limited classroom time as a substitute teacher did not allow for an extended interaction with the two focus students, those students' surveys were analyzed individually. The researcher was interested in the possible effect that family financial situation had on student response. One of the focus students was from an affluent background and the other from a family of poverty. However, the responses of the two students were so similar, and the data pool was so small in regard to this secondary question that it was dropped from further consideration.

Due to concerns over a possible backlash by teachers, the self-assessment aspect of this study was eliminated, as well as the para-educator assessment. The goal of this study was to analyze the impact, if any, that teacher immediacy had on student motivation, and the researcher decided to base this study on student perception alone. Further extensions of the current study will gather additional data from teachers.

Conclusion

According to this study, there is a strong correlation between the teacher immediacy behaviors used in classrooms and the motivation of the students who are in those classes. Students notice and pick up on verbal and non-verbal behaviors exhibited by teachers.

When teachers consistently use behaviors that decrease the physical or psychological distance between the teachers and their students, those teachers help create a learning environment in which students are more interested, engaged and motivated.

The teacher immediacy behaviors that were most motivating to the students in this study were - smiling, the use of humor, the use of the students' first names by the teacher, the teacher asking for student input and opinions, and consistent eye contact by the teacher toward both individual students and the entire class.

When discussing the survey results with the focus group of students, nearly all students were adamant that they could 'sense' whether a teacher liked them or not, whether a teacher was comfortable around them, and whether a teacher enjoyed what he or she did.

This group of focus students agreed strongly that a teacher who was friendly and warm created a much more motivating classroom atmosphere. Students stated that a teacher's immediacy behaviors were a much greater motivator than the content of a course and that their perception of a subject was changed – either for better or worse – by the warmth of a teacher.

This research is vital. In this day and age of data-driven instruction, pacing guides and scribed teacher texts, the human connection is forgotten. Teaching is a human endeavor and our students are living beings. Without a consistent use of immediacy skills and behaviors, teachers' effectiveness will always be less than it could be. The results of this study are a loud reminder of the importance of this human connection between teacher and student.

—————————

References for this study are in a separate section at the end of the book.

Chapter Eighteen: Leading and Managing

"Leadership is not about a title or designation. It's about impact, influence and inspiration."
Robin S. Sharma

Management, as an idea, is built on the assumption that people need prodding by reward or punishment to accomplish things. Without a firm and reliable guide, we would become lost. I don't think we are wired that way. People are wired to be active, engaged, curious and to get things done. Have you seen a young child who was not curious and active? Nope. What happens to them as they age?

Management often crushes this spirit. We don't all of a sudden stop being curious or creative at the age of 15 - we are often 'educated' out of it. We must resist the temptation to control people and do everything we can to reawaken their deep-seated sense of autonomy. The opposite of autonomy is control. Control leads to compliance – autonomy leads to engagement.

People love to have enough freedom to try new things. If that is stifled, mediocrity settles in and the best people leave. The most creative and engaging people have minds that HAVE TO work! If you force a creative thinker to comply and conform you will lose him. The lack of individual discretion at work is the main explanation for declining job satisfaction.

Management still revolves around supervision, evaluations and if/then rewards. A strict policy that forces teachers to follow pacing guides and scripted lessons 'with fidelity' is like forcing an artist to paint a designated picture starting at 9:00 a.m. using specified brushes, paints and colors and requiring the painting to be completed by 3:00 p.m.

I have written over a hundred songs and parodies for my presentation business, for fun and for other events. Occasionally someone asks me to write a song for a specific person and with a specific theme. Those songs take a lot longer to complete and often become rather tedious.

Teachers need some freedom and discretion or they will all leave, except for the poor ones who don't like to think anyway. If an administrator doesn't listen to her people, it won't be long before no one is speaking. Sadly, many leaders like it that way.

Here are some ideas to improve the culture in your organization:

1. Involve others in goal setting.

2. Use non-controlling language (instead of you NEED TO, you should say "think about" or "consider.")

3. Start using 'we' more than 'I' and 'us' more than 'me.' 'We' teams are best.

4. Gather your team and ask – what is our school's purpose? If people don't know why they are doing what they are doing, how can you expect them to be motivated to do it? But mission statements alone will not change a school. The talk has to be walked in every hall from the top down. 'People don't buy what we say, they buy what we do.'

5. How about giving people (teachers/students) 10% or so of time to think, create and dream? Why can't we have in-services that give teachers time to dream up new ideas.

6. Lead with questions, not answers. . . engage in dialogue and debate, not coercion . . . evaluate problems without blame . . . make it easy for employees to speak up when they see a problem.

7. Make sure meetings actually matter. Use meetings for dialogue and debate. Meetings don't have to prove anything, especially the power of the boss.

Questions for Teachers

1. Am I giving students any autonomy over what, how and when to do their homework?
2. Does this assignment promote mastery by offering an engaging task?
3. Do my students understand the purpose for this?
4. Could I have a FEDEX day with my kids?

5. What do my grades represent? Good grades are often a reward for compliance – they have little to do with learning. Makes sure you know what your grades represent.

6. Praise specific things. Praise in private. Only give praise when there is a good reason for it.

President Lincoln was self-confident enough to surround himself with people who were better than he was in certain areas. Lincoln genuinely listened to other people's points of view, which helped him form more complex opinions of his own. Lincoln gave credit where it was due and wasn't afraid to take the blame.

Do rewards motivate people? Sure! They motivate people to get rewards!

Mastery is the desire to get better and better at something that matters. A very small percentage of people are highly engaged at work. The reason is simple; we focus far too much on compliance and far too little on engagement.

Autotelic activity – FLOW – happens when people are so enthralled in what they are doing that they seem to be in a trance. Time passes quickly and self-consciousness dissolves. Athletes, artists, rock climbers, people with hobbies, etc. - many have been studied and asked about their grasp of 'flow,' but few could explain how it felt in the moment. A runner's high is a physical manifestation of this idea. When time flies by, the challenge in your activity is perfect - not too hard, not too easy. In this FLOW, the goals are clear – climb the mountain, hit the ball, mold the clay, etc. and the paths toward those goals are interesting and purposeful.

After FLOW, GRIT is what gets us to master something. Sticking to it – day after day. Effort gives meaning to life – effort means you care about something, that something is important to you and you are willing to work for it. What moments produce FLOW in your life? Where were you? What were you doing? Who was with you?

Leadership has nothing to do with rank. It has to do with skill and choice. People at the 'top' are not necessarily leaders, they are authorities. The opposite is true, people at the bottom who have no authority may be the true leaders. The reason? Those people are more focused on others than themselves.

Real leaders sacrifice for others and that results in their workers doing the same. A good leader is not a 'Super Hero' or 'Stand and Command' position. Great leaders see around corners and shape the future instead of reacting to it. Great leaders have a diversity of workers and they listen to them. Great leaders can abandon the past when necessary.

Head count doesn't matter as much as heart count. As I mentioned earlier, people today want value and worth more than rewards. They want to impact the world. It is essential that today's leaders understand this shift in purpose and learn how to draw the best from their employees, especially their younger ones. How can this happen? A quick look at the foundational aspects of effective leadership is a starting point.

A leader's role is to drive debate, not always force consensus.

Leadership is the secret sauce – but it is a different kind of leadership than what we currently think of when we think of leaders. Leading is about creating the space where people are willing and able to do their work and solve the problems that arise.

Effective leaders build a sense of community. They create a world where people want to belong and design a workplace where people interact. Imagine a place where everyone can give notes to the boss - where minority voices are heard. Effective leaders give credit to others and take the blame whenever possible. Talented people don't want to always just follow a boss - they want to do some of their own thinking too. Most workers enjoy accomplishing something worthwhile.

The best leaders connect and work with the bottom and the top. They are role models, human glue and are never a dictator of viewpoints. They even hire people who argue with them to draw out disagreements.

Many leaders are used to setting goals and making sure no one deviates from their plans. The problem in that is that everyone is looking at the boss. It should be opposite. Invert the pyramid. Decrease the power of the few and give it to the many. Our role as leaders is to set the stage, not perform on it. Create the space where everyone's slice of creativity is harnessed and turned into a collective genius.

In their book, 'Flex,' Jane Hyun and Audrey S. Lee do a great job of describing and defining effective leadership. Their concepts of the 'power gap' and 'flexing' are very helpful here.

According to Hyun and Lee, the 'Power Gap' is the social distance that separates individuals from those in positions of authority; whether in formal or informal situations. Gender, age, culture and education are examples of variables that divide.

'Flexing' is the ability to adapt how one communicates, relates and responds to others in a manner that takes into account the power gap and an understanding of status differences.

Effective leaders understand this power gap and learn to 'flex.' They can 'see' the differences between their positions as leaders and that of their other team members without bias. Great leaders do not require others to adapt to their styles, but instead adapt their style in order to meet their team members partway and bridge the gap between them.

It takes courage to be a leader who inspires others to contribute their very best. Creating an environment of trust is not easy. It involves a heartfelt belief and constant commitment. The way you handle the power gap between you and your employees can make or break your company. Talking about differences is hard. The phrase, "I don't see color," can deny the value of other cultures.

We need an insatiable curiosity about the stories, perspectives and motivations of others. A great leader is able to work and communicate effortlessly with many types of people who are different from him/herself.

Hyun and Lee identify several leadership styles that relate to this concept of the power gap:* If you are a school leader, principal or other education leader, look for yourself here.

The Blindsided Manager – You don't really like working with people different from you. You aren't even aware of the power gap that exists between you and your employees. Because of that, you don't even notice your lack of ability in closing the gap. You just follow the course and avoid any unnecessary or uncomfortable issues. "No news is good news," in regard to your people. If they haven't complained, you must be doing something right. When conflict does arise, you try to avoid it, point fingers or shift the attention away from it.

The Judging Manager – You find people who are different from you as annoying. You judge or resent those who have different thoughts. When push comes to shove, you know YOUR way is the right one. You expect your team to conform to your style without question.

The Golden Rule Manager – Diversity training and experience has taught you that it is safest to treat everybody exactly the same. While people are different, we are all human on the inside. Differences are deemphasized and they don't really matter in the work place. Subconsciously, you use your own 'background and value system' as the template for managing people fairly.

The Fluent Leader – This leader understands the power gap and is valuing and respecting of everyone. If this is you, congratulations. You have learned how to lead without forcing compliance or micromanaging. Your people enjoy working with you and your trust in them gives them great comfort. You can adapt and 'flex' to meet any situation without blowing a gasket.

When managers choose to close the gap and meet their employees partway, they are not giving away authority and respect. Closing the power gap doesn't make the leader vulnerable; it fact, it usually does the opposite, creating trust and communication where before there was only conflict and poor performance. Understanding the power gap and managing it is one of your top priorities as a leader. Without those things, you will fail.

Remember that an 'open door' policy often shuts people out. An open-door policy puts the onus on the employee to identify the problem and come to you to speak out. Many won't do that. Leaders have to be the ones seeking out the problems and thoughts. They must catch most problems before they hatch into larger ones.

Here is a quick list of effective leadership skills and strategies I have collected over the years. If you are a leader, use it as a checklist. If you have a poor boss, share this section anonymously with her.

1. Start with authenticity. Show others who you are and what you value and then extend your curiosity to others.

2. Good leaders find ways to remove barriers that exist when working across cultural, generational and gender differences.

3. Leaders need to learn to recognize what they DON'T know. Leaders don't have to know it all. They just need to create a climate that brings out the best in their people, so they are willing to try new things.

4. The most effective leaders are able to assess their mistakes honestly. They work hard to improve themselves instead of looking for a scapegoat or trying to minimize mistakes to look good to colleagues and superiors.

5. Effective leaders constantly sense the 'feel' of their people and think ahead.

6. Effective leaders have a people sense. They can gauge the mood and attitudes of their people. They address issues before they become enraged.

7. A great leader looks in the mirror to find responsibility for poor results and areas to improve. "It was my fault." A great leader doesn't look out the window to blame others or bad luck. But, they do look out the window to give credit when good things happen or when a spell of 'good luck' comes. "It was all my people- there are amazing people here."

8. A great leader is a strange blend of personal humility and professional ambition. Usually quiet, introspective and reserved, often even shy.

9. Strong leaders know that people are more valuable than programs. The pressure to perform in a great organization doesn't come from the top down, it comes from a horizontal challenge between colleagues. Great teaching teams challenge each other. A principal wouldn't even be necessary.

10. Leaders must be able to confront the most brutal facts of their current situation.

11. Great leaders ask many more questions than giving answers. They don't come into any meeting with a predetermined plan or answer. They ask questions and listen first. "How are things going?"

12. Outstanding leaders are open to failures and do autopsies without blaming others. "Wow, that didn't work. Why? Now, let's give it another look."

That's a challenging list for me and probably for most leaders. I wish I could remember the articles, blogs, books, videos and people from which I gathered it all.

As I conclude this chapter on leadership, I have a few requests for all leaders.

Spending time and energy trying to motivate people or build a 'team' through goofy team-building activities is a WASTE of time and effort. The wrong people will love them, but the right people are already self-motivated and see the shallowness. You will end up demotivating your best people which is the last thing you want.

Great leaders also shouldn't talk much about themselves, they should talk much more about their organization and the contributions of their people. Great leaders are described by their people as being, quiet, humble, modest, reserved, shy, gracious. mild-mannered, understated, etc. The idea of servant leadership is found here.

Great leaders also have an almost fanatical drive to produce results, to accomplish something and to get better. They will do what they have to do. They work harder than all of their people. They make the tough decisions. Don't think a servant leader is a pushover or a sissy. He does what needs to be done, but personal ego is out of any decision.

Chapter Nineteen: Triggering a Revolution

"When I think back on all the crap I learned in high school, it's a wonder I can think at all." - Paul Simon

Paul Simon wrote "Kodachrome" back in 1972, but in many ways his words fit better 40 years later. Undoubtedly, schools have improved in many ways since my eight-track tape deck played Simon and Garfunkel's music. Teachers are working harder. Administrators are pushing teachers further. Parents are demanding more. There is more student-driven data than ever and there are clearly defined standards and curriculum on every wall.

Schools are producing students who often score well on assessments, and those who cannot, get special incentives and help. For the most part, our current education system is doing what it is supposed to be doing - producing young people who are increasingly able to check the right boxes on computerized tests.

I wonder what the Paul Simons of today say about schools. Given Simon's creative, artistic gifts, it should not be difficult to understand his perspective. The spontaneity, sensitivity and sincerity of artists run counter to current educational paths. Ponder this question - Do you think teaching is an 'art' or is it a 'science?'

Elliot W. Eisner, one of the most highly regarded leaders in the field of school curriculum, discussed this question in his powerful book on education, *The Educational Imagination.* Speaking of the science of teaching, he uses the words, 'cold and calculated,' while addressing the artistic nature with 'passionate and personal.'[xlix]   Although Eisner's book was written twenty years ago, his words should sound loud warnings today.

In a previous chapter, I mentioned that humanities and art classes are often seen as being somehow 'less' than real school. Physical education classes are being shortened or even cut from schools across the nation, while extra prescriptions of reading and math courses are substituted in their place.

Reading and math are at the top of the curricular food chain and everything else is of much less importance. Measurable assessment data and scientific analysis of student skills and scores drive decisions. The words rigor, objectives, benchmarks, data, and assessments echo in staff meetings everywhere.

We study education like we study the braking distance of new cars. Teachers are evaluated on student data and classrooms function like laboratories. Human judgments and teacher discernment are not needed in a world of objective tests and data-driven decisions. Education has become impersonal.

Eisner says it best: "The science of education believes that the only thing that counts in education is how students behave, not what they believe, think, feel or experience. It is odd that therapists are required to develop personal sensitivity as a tool to help people grow, while teachers are not. Both are involved in educating people, facilitating others development. We remember our most influential teachers not just by what they did, but by who they were, how they inspired us. It is their qualities as human beings that profoundly affect us."[d]

We cannot forget that there is more to effective teaching than writing objectives and recording assessment performances. The ability to connect with students, value them and inspire them is just as important, if not more.

Humans are not impersonal creatures. Like plants, humans are organisms that flourish if the environment is right. An environment that is cold, objective and data-driven is not a place where humans flourish. People are not machines.

What makes us human is our ability to imagine things, dream things, feel things, and to have compassion for other humans. We sing, dance, play music, and paint pictures. We run, jump, act and build skyscrapers. Some of us have special gifts in these artistic areas and find tremendous satisfaction and fulfillment when we use them. So do many of our students.

The boy who has trouble reading might have incredible eye/hand coordination, excelling in sports and games. The girl who struggles with math can sing like an angel. But what are we doing in schools today? Because both of these fictional students fail to meet a certain level on a major assessment in reading and math, we remove them from physical education and choir and give them another dose of 'core' classes.

District budgets tighten and where are the first cuts made? The answer is obvious and is a source of frustration for many of my friends and colleagues who are excellent teachers in these 'non-core' subject areas. We will pay a huge price if we continue deemphasizing the arts.

The arts are how humans make connections between the outer world and their own inner world.[li] The more we slide arts to the back burners, the less our students are able to engage with and express what is inside of them.

We must remember that education is personal and the arts are a vital part of an effective education. If students feel education is impersonal they will turn away from it. The reason remedial education works is because of its one-on-one contact. MTSS (Multi-Tiered System of Support) works for the same reasons, although it is incredibly data-driven. Students need personal contact. We know that. So why do we make classes so impersonal?

There are teachers who can go through an entire semester without knowing the names of their students. I am not just talking about university professors in large lecture classes. Although we seldom admit it, education rolls along on the rails of conformity.

Students must conform and so do teachers. Those that cannot or do not, pay the price. I am challenging you to take a step or two outside the box of educational conformity.

Effective and influential teachers find a way to help students understand themselves. These teachers know that students learn more than they are taught and teachers teach more than they realize.

Exceptional teachers understand the difference between

education, schooling and learning. They provide students with opportunities to search their minds and hearts. There are some very important 'hidden' lessons our young people need from teachers today.

Today's students need to be still. Some need to learn how to be still. They need time to think. Most need to learn how to think. They need time to reflect. Many of them do not know how to do any of those things.

Students in our classrooms today have grown up in a loud, fast, busy and connected world. Youth today have been 'plugged in' since birth. They have been sheltered, overprotected and coddled.[lii] I recommend another fantastic book here: Tim Elmore's *Generation iY: Our Last Chance to Save Their Future*. Mr. Elmore's book opened my eyes to the struggles our current generation of youngsters' face.

Elmore writes that we have forgotten that America was built on opportunity, failure and determination. If our students do not learn to think for themselves or learn how to persevere when trials come, they will have a lot of trouble coping with life.

In record numbers, adult children are moving back home with their parents because they cannot hold a job or are not able to deal with the frustrations of life.

Many of today's youth have had relatively easy lives. When things get a little tough, they give up more quickly. Although they have developed an amazing ability to multi-task, they have great difficult focusing on one task for very long. Students of today are about interaction. Many cannot sit still for more than a few minutes.

Students in our classrooms today can be careless and rude. Some of the underdeveloped virtues of this generation are obvious to teachers: patience, compromise, responsibility, work ethic and perseverance, to name just a few. Our young people need teachers who accept, support, and guide and encourage them while at the same time demanding greatness.

I leave you with some lyrics from the song, "For Good," from the musical *Wicked*. These words reflect the heart of effective and influential teaching and they challenge us with their truth.

> *"It well may be that we will never meet again in this lifetime. So, let me say before we part,*
>
> *So much of me is made from what I learned from you and you'll be with me like a handprint on my heart.*
>
> *And now whatever way our stories end I know you have re-written mine by being my friend.*
>
> *Like a ship blown from its mooring by a wind off the sea like a seed dropped by a sky bird in a distant wood, who can say if I've been changed for the better? But because I knew you, I have been changed for good."*

Please, keep making ripples - inspiring ones, challenging ones, and encouraging ones. The ripples you create today will touch my path tomorrow. Thank you for that.

Other References: Chapter Eighteen

Elmore, Tim. *Generation iY: Our Last Chance to Save Their Future.* Poet Gardener Publishing. 2010. Print.

Schwartz, Stephen. "For Good." *Wicked.* 2003. CD.

Simon, Paul. "Kodachrome." *There Goes Rhymin' Simon.* 1973. CD.

Robinson, Sir Ken. *Schools are Killing Creativity.* TEDTalks. 2006. www.ted.com. June 2010. Video.

Chapter Twenty: Gathering the Pearls

"I did then what I knew how to do. Now that I know better, I do better."
Maya Angelou

I hope there was something in this book that challenged you, resonated with you or even better, struck a nerve. Although you surely didn't agree with everything I shared, I do hope you found a couple helpful ideas or strategies along the way.

This final chapter is a compilation of my keys to effective teaching and career-changing work in education. Most of the following were discussed previously in this book; however, because the process of writing a book is lengthy, I had time to include a few 'new' extra pearls.

Please use this final chapter as a review, a reminder or a checklist. If you are a busy educator and don't have time to read the entire book, at least read this chapter. Share it with a friend.

Laughlin's Keys to Effective Teaching

1. Know Yourself

   Strengths, weaknesses, personality type, learning style, multiple intelligences, triggers

2. Know Your Mission

   Purpose, passion, mission statement, eulogy skills

3. Know Your Stuff

   Job expectations, content, curriculum, community

4. Know and Value People (Be curious about others)

   Perspectives, listen well, get others to tell their story, respect, humility, being intentional, taking time

5. Value Connections/Relationships as Much as Content

   Deposit in people's lives, ask for help, compliment others, notice something, sharpen teacher immediacy behaviors

6. Value Emotion as Much as Intellect

   Emotional Quotient, motivation and learning, it's what students 'feel' while they learn, vulnerability, empathy

7. Value Respect

   Give respect to get respect, respect must be modeled, servant leadership, classroom management starts here, all people involved, demanding respect can backfire, everyone wants to be respected

8. Establish Procedures

   All the classroom things that save time down the road; tardy policy, seating, homework, fire drill, restrooms, late work, handing in work, active shooter plan, etc.

9. Establish Safety

Maslow's needs, physical and emotional, classroom community/family, honesty, comfort levels

10. Recognize the Science and Art of Questioning/Listening

Listen to really listen, prompt critical thought, two-question rule (always ask at least one follow-up question), push deeper, Bloom's taxonomy, WHY more important than what, when, where and who, etc.

11. Recognize the Science and Art of Teaching

Pedagogical practices/strategies, planning, researching, instructing, learning styles, brain breaks, group work, individual work, incorporating technology, etc.

12. Recognize the Science and Art of Motivation

Intrinsic vs. extrinsic, growth and fixed mindsets, FLOW, autonomy, giving options, purpose, levels of challenge

13. Develop Critical Thought

Bloom's, cognitive ease vs. strain, mindset, brain research, debates, opinions, life applications, current events, various perspectives

14. Develop Character

Modeling is crucial, respectful/caring community, teach societal norms, practice constantly, this is a constant undercurrent, NOT a 'canned' curriculum or 'forced' course

15. Develop Climate & Culture

Build people up, look for good, expect to make a difference, guide others, helping, caring, empathy, leadership matters, leadership characteristics, etc.

There you have them – my fifteen keys to education. I'd like to say I have mastered them all but every student I ever taught would tell you differently. I just keep learning and growing each class and each year. My mistakes and failures - and there are plenty - provide a constant source of opportunity for improvement. My goal is that the final class I teach will be my best.

My greatest desire is that ALL my students know and feel that I care about them deeply, personally and eternally and that I let them tell their stories. Perhaps one day a few of those stories will include me in a background role. That is the legacy we can all hope for – to have made a difference. We can do this. We are educators.

Citations

[i] "Top Five Reasons Why Teacher Turnover is Rising." Huff Post Education. 2011. www.huffingtonpost.com/2011/08/11/top-5-reasons-why-teacher_n_924428.html. Web.

[ii] Whitaker, Todd. What Great Principals Do Differently: Fifteen Things That Matter Most. Larchmont, NY. Eye on Education, 2002. Print.

[iii] Whitaker, Todd. What Great Teachers Do Differently: Fifteen Things That Matter Most. Larchmont, NY. Eye on Education, 2003. Print.

[iv] "*Mr. Laughlin on Live with Regis & Kelly*. *Live on Regis and Kelly TV Show*. 2010. www.youtube.com/watch?v=TYtpzGZ8774. Video.

[v] Colvin, Geoff. *Talent Is Overrated*. Portfolio Hardcover. 2012. Print.

[vi] "A History of Compulsory Education Laws." *Fastback Series, No. 75. Bicentennial Series*. www.eric.ed.gov. 1976. Print.

[vii] Thomas N. Bonner, "Sputniks and the Educational Crisis in America." *The Journal of Higher Education*, 1957. Print.

[viii] Bonner, Thomas. *The Journal of Higher Education, 1957*. Print. September 2011.

[ix] Millburn, John. "Kansas audit pegs cost of new ed standards," 2012. www.hutchnews.com. Web. January 2013.

[x] Delisle, Jason. "Putting a number of federal education spending," (2013). http://economix.blogs.nytimes.com. Web. March 2013.

[xi] Covey, Stephen R. *Seven Habits of Highly Effective People*. Free Press, (1989). Print.

[xii] Bangayan, Samantha. "Two reasons you need a personal mission statement." Yellow Brick Road (2011). www.yellowbrickroad.com. Web. November 2012.

[xiii] Tieger, Paul. "Take our free personalitytype.com assessment." PersonalityType.com. www.personalitytype.com/quiz. Web. January 2012.

[xiv] Haynes, Judie. *"Teach to Students' Learning Styles."* EverythingESL.net. www.everythingesl.net. Web. March 2012.

[xv] Terry, Alice. *More Life Through Management.* Creative Teaching Press. Print. 1998.

[xvi] Marzano, Robert J., Daisy E. Pickering, and Jane Pollock. *Classroom Instruction That Works. Virginia: ASCD,* 2001. Print.

[xvii] Bowen, Will. *Complaint Free Relationships: Transforming Your Life One Relationship at a Time.* Random House Audio. 2009. Print.

[xviii] Kerman, S., Kimball, T., and Martin, M. *Teacher Expectations and Student Achievement.* Phi Delta Kappa International Inc., 1980. Print.

[xix] Chiu, L. H. and Tulley, M. "Student preferences of teacher discipline styles." *Journal of Instructional Psychology, 1997.* 168-175. March 2012.

[xx] Fay, Jim. *Love & Logic.* Love and Logic Press, (1995). Print.

[xxi] Freire, Paulo. *Pedagogy of the Oppressed.* New York: Bloomsbury Academic, 30th Anniversary Edition, 2000. Print.

[xxii] Hendricks, Howard. *Teaching to Change Lives: Seven Proven Ways to Make Your Teaching Come Alive.* Colorado Springs, Colorado: Multnomah Books, 1998. Print.

[xxiii] Wong, Harry. *The First Days of School.* Mountain View, California: Harry K. Wong's Publications. 2004. Print.

[xxiv] Heide, Florence Parry. *The Shrinking of Treehorn*. Holiday House, Reprint 1992. Print.

[xxv] Geisel, Theodor Seuss. *The Sneetches*. Random House, 1961. Print.

[xxvi] Pfister, Marcus. *The Rainbow Fish*. North-South Books, 1995. Print.

[xxvii] Tate, Marcia. *Worksheets Don't Grow Dendrites*. Corwin. Second Edition, 2010. Print.

[xxviii] Wong, Harry. *The First Days of School*. Mountain View, California: Harry K. Wong's Publications. 2004. Print.

[xxix] Whitaker, Todd. *What Great Teachers Do Differently: Fifteen Things That Matter Most*. Larchmont, NY. Eye on Education, 2003. Print.

[xxx] Payne, Ruby. *Framework for Understanding Poverty*. Highlands, Texas: Aha Process Inc., Fourth Edition, 2005. Print.

[xxxi] Smith, M. K. "Learning Theory." *The Encyclopedia of Informal Education*. 2003. http://infed.org/mobi/learning-theory-models-product-and-process/. Web. June 2012.

[xxxii] Paul, Annie Murphy. "What we learn before we are born." TEDtalks. www.ted.com. 2011. Video. June 2012.

[xxxiii] Faculty Development and Instructional Design Center. Northern Illinois University. "Teaching with the Revised Bloom's Taxonomy." www.niu.edu. 2009. Web. July 2012.

[xxxiv] Krathwol, David R. "A Revision of Bloom's Taxonomy. *Theory Into Practice*. Ohio State University. 2002. www.unco.edu. July 2012.

[xxxv] Block, Phil. "Needs Analysis, Part One." www.philblock.info/hitkb/n/needs_analysis1.html. Web. July 2012.

[xxxvi] McGee, Patricia. "Learning Objects: *Bloom's Taxonomy* and Deeper Learning Principles." *faculty.coehd.utsa.edu/pmcgee/nlii/lobloomsmcgee.doc*. Web. August 2012.

[xxxvii] Ad Council. "United Negro College Fund." http://www.adcouncil.org/Our-Work/The-Classics/United-Negro-College-Fund. 1972. Television/Web. August 2012.

[xxxviii] Clark, Don. "Formal and Informal Learning." *Knowledge Jump*. www.knowledgejump.com. 2007. Web. August 2012.

[xxxix] Knowles, Malcom. "Informal Adult Education: A Guide For Administrators, Leaders, And Teachers." University Of Michigan: Association Press, 1950. Web. April 2012.

[xl] Clark, Don. "Formal and Informal Learning." *Knowledge Jump*. www.knowledgejump.com. 2007. Web. August 2012.

[xli] President's Council of Economic Advisors. "Preparing the Workers of Today for the Jobs of Tomorrow." *The White House*. 2009. www.whitehouse.gov. Web. April 2012.

[xlii] Kant, Immanuel. "What is Enlightenment?" *Berlin Monthly*. 1784. Print. September 2012.

[xliii] Hurt, Jeff. "Ten Brain-Based Learning Laws that Trump Traditional Education." *Velvet Chainsaw*. 2012. Web. October 2012.

[xliv] Mager, Robert. *Making Instruction Work*. Center for Effective Performance. Second Edition, 1997. Print.

[xlv] Florida Center for Instructional Technology. "Formative vs. Summative Assessments." fcit.usf.edu. Web. September 2012.

[xlvi] Tuckman, Bruce. "Forming, Storming, Norming, Performing." 1965. *Princeton University*. Print. October 2012.

[xlvii] Alcott, Bobby. Image source: *Flickr*. Web. October 2012.

[xlviii] Lennon, John, "Revolution." *The White Album, The Beatles.* 1968. Record. October 2012.

[xlix] Eisner, Elliot W. *The Educational Imagination.* New York: Pearson. 1979. Print.

[l] Eisner, Elliot W. *The Educational Imagination.* New York: Pearson. 1979. Page 322. Print.

[li] Robinson, Sir Ken. *Schools are Killing Creativity.* TEDTalks. 2006. www.ted.com. June 2010. Video.

[lii] Elmore, Tim. *Generation iY: Our Last Chance to Save Their Future.* Poet Gardener Publishing. 2010. Print.

References from the Chapter Seventeen Research Study

Andersen, J.F. (1978). The relationship between teacher immediacy and teacher effectiveness. Unpublished doctoral dissertation, West Virginia University, Morgantown.

Butland, M. J., & Beebe, S. A. (1992). Teacher immediacy and power in the classroom: The application of implicit communication theory. Paper presented at the Annual Meeting of the International Communication Association, Miami, FL.

Cherry, K. (n.d.). Motivation: The Psychological Factors That Guide Us. Retrieved February 18, 2015, from http://psychology.about.com

Christensen, L. J., Curley, K. E., Marquez, E. M., & Menzel, K. E. (1995, November). *Classroom situations which lead to student participation.* Paper presented at the 1995 annual meeting of the Speech Communication Association, San Antonio, TX.

Christophel, D. M. (1990). The relationships among teacher immediacy behaviors, student motivation and learning. Communication Education, 39, 323- 340.

Gorham, J. (1988). The Relationship Between Verbal Teacher Immediacy and Student Learning. *Communication Education, 37,* 40-53.

Keith, P., & Wetherbee, M. (1995). *Identifying unmotivated students: Planning school-wide interventions.*

Lamm (2011). Teacher Immediacy. (n.d.). Retrieved February 18, 2015, from http://blogs.nvcc.edu/cetl/2011/12/09/teacher-immediacy/

Lovett (2014). Identify Problem - Teaching Excellence & Educational Innovation - Carnegie Mellon University. (n.d.). Retrieved February 18, 2015.

Martin, M. (n.d.). Students' Motives for Communicating with Their Instructors and Affective and Cognitive Learning. *Psychological Reports,* 830-830.

Marzano (2003). Membership. Retrieved February 18, 2015, from leadership/sept03/vol61/num01

McNamee, S., & Miller, R. (2004). *The meritocracy myth.* Lanham, Md.: Rowman & Littlefield

Postman, N., & Weingartner, C. (1969). *Teaching as a subversive activity.* New York: Delacorte Press.

Richmond, V.P. (2002). Teacher nonverbal immediacy: Uses and outcomes. In J.L. Chesebro & J.C.

Robinson, K., & Aronica, L. (n.d.). *Finding your element: How to discover your talents and passions and transform your life.* Rubin, R. B.,

Palmgreen, P., & Sypher, H. E. (Eds.). (1994). Communication research measures: A sourcebook. New York: Guilford Press.

Velez, J., & Cano, J. (n.d.). The Relationship Between Teacher Immediacy and Student Motivation. *Journal of Agricultural Education,* 76-86.

Weiner, B. (1992). Human Motivation: Metaphors, theories and research. Newbury Park, CA: Sage.

Witt, P. L., Wheeless, L. R., & Allen, M. (2004). A meta-analytical review of the relationship between teacher immediacy and student learning. Communication Monographs, 71(2), 184-207.

Other Resources:

Hyun, Jane, and Audrey S. Lee. Flex: The New Playbook for Managing across Differences. Harper Business, 2014.

Brown, Brene'. Braving the Wilderness: The Quest for True Belonging and the Courage to Stand Alone. Random House, 2017.

Meyer, Danny. Setting the Table: The Transforming Power of Hospitality in Business. Harper, 2008.

Postman, Neil, and Charles Weingartner. Teaching as a Subversive Activity. Penguin Books, 1972.

Collins, Jim. Good to Great. Harper Business, 2001.

The Golden Circle – Simon Sinek (video) www.ted.com%2ftalks%2fsimon_sinek_how_great_leaders_inspire_action&p=DevEx,5072.1.

Special thanks to Marty Hays, who has inspired me to become a more effective educator through his research, insight and challenges.

Also, a huge thank you to ALL my teaching colleagues over the years. I'm sure something you've shared with me at some point is in this book.

Thanks to Mark Jarvis and the Butler Community College Faculty Development Team, for encouraging and challenging me with fresh new strategies and research.

Notes

Made in the USA
Middletown, DE
30 August 2019